JOHN BOLSTRIDGE 75 years old and has lived his life with dyslexia, a learning disorder. In 2010 after losing his wife to breast cancer, started to put down onto a computer what was inside of his head.

Although John fount storytelling easy the grammar and spelling he used in writing would make the average person have a good laugh, But John continued even with the disability of being dyslexic, he continued.

All that John hopes is that readers give him a chance after learning and reading this, and the disability trying to overcome the dyslexia, if just one person with dyslexia takes up the challenge to author a book, then my goal would have been reached.

Thanks for taking the time to read this, and the story that follows.

John Bolstridge.

PROLOGUE

This story is about a young man who becomes famous for doing what all young souls want to do and that is, to become.
Famous, "What do you mean I hear you shouting."

Well sit back, and read on, what you are about to read is straight out of a fairytale book, we have all read about Superhero`s like Superman and kryptonite, the hulk, batman, and Robin, well this story is on the same lines but brought up to date in these Modern days with computers and Artificial intelligence, AI in short.

Even our inventers and computer programmers are saying that AI, is fast overtaking us humans, and are frightened at what AI, is becoming. Well you are about to find out, our story starts with young William Drake a young student attending Baltimore State Academy, we pick up the story one Summers day Will up early for as well as last day at school before the Summer holidays, and most of all it was wills Birthday.

THE GIFT FROM A.I.

CHAPTER ONE

William up early and in the bathroom cleaning his teeth, with his Mum shouting up to him from bottom of the stairs.

"William are you up yet." William shouts back down telling his Mum.

"Yes Mum just cleaning my teeth, will be right down." William grumbling under his breath saying.

"What time does my Mum want me to get up, I thought I was early with it only half-past six."

William out of the bathroom dresses into his school uniform, saying.

"Roll on last time for six weeks that I will be readying myself in school uniform." William going down and into the kitchen where is Mum was cooking breakfast, but Will had noticed the cards and a cake on the table, with his Mum turning and wishing Will a happy sixteenth Birthday.

"Happy Birthday William sixteen to-day." Wills Mum coming over and giving William a big kiss and telling him.

"Your father had to go to work early this morning, he says his birthday wishes and will catch you later after school when he gets back from the station.
Wills Dad was an Officer in the local Police force, and missed his Sons birthday with having to go to work that morning at five am, for his start of shift.
William eating his breakfast and opening his cards and most of the cards held Money, Will looking at all of the dollars piled high on the table tells his Mum.

"Boy its great not being a kid anymore for look Mum I`m rich."
"It is nice at your age but remember the older you get the less cards and money you will get, mark my words Son."

"It's nice any way." William counting the dollars, with his Mum telling him.
"Maybe we will take you to the mall later with your Dad, and you can treat yourself to something there."
Eight pm the front doorbell goes and William jumping up and telling his Mum.
"I`ll go it must be Bobby." William goes to the front door and sure enough it was Bobby

Williams school mate who was in the same class as William.

"Hi Bobby, you're early, why is that." Asking William.

"Well I wanted to give you this, my Mum told me to give it to you now instead on the way to school."

"Thanks Mate come on in and I will put this card you gave me with the rest." William and Bobby going back into the kitchen with Bobby saying hello to Mrs Drake.

"Hello Bobby hopes you are well, and less of the Mrs, its Mavis to Williams friends." Bobby smiling at Williams Mum and commenting on how many cards William had, with William telling Bobby.

"I`ve had a lot from my uncles and Aunties." William picking up his school case up of the chair and telling his Mum.

"I`m off now Mum see you when I get back this afternoon."

"Take care William and be safe out there with Bobby."

"We`ll be fine Mrs Drake." Well the look of sternness at what Bobby said with Bobby apologising saying.

"Sorry Mavis, bye see you later." William and Bobby go off running down the path and down to the end of the road where there was about a dozen other boys and girls waiting for the school bus, William and Bobby stand there and Bobby ask Will.

"What have you on this morning at School.

"Firstly it's my favoured subject computer programming, then down to the sports field for American football, then this afternoon I`ve mock exams, what about yourself Bobby."

"No other than English and Maths."

"Sorry about that Bobby I hate maths and English boring subjects."

"I don`t mind them, it's better than doing RE,I hate that sort of thing."

"Me too you can see why they dropped it from a full lesson, with having multi diversions in these modern times." They had just finished talking when the bus pulls up and they all climb aboard for the short journey to school. They arrive and William tells Bobby he will see him later as they go their separate ways for Bobby was in the fifteen class as William was in the sixth form. William goes into class and sits at his computer when into the classroom comes Mr Davis.

"Good morning class, hopes you are all well and ready for today's lesson on how to build a programme to run your needs for business accounts, firstly turn on your computers."

"And by the way let's all congratulate William Drake on his sixteenth birthday to-day." They all give William a clap and sing happy birthday to him. William is taking the applause and clapping in, and sitting back down onto the screen of his computer comes the voice of Olivia the new windows voice, which replaces the outdated version Cortana.

"Good morning William and congratulations on your sixteenth Birthday."

"Who said that."

"Why it was I Olivia, Look at the bottom of your screen I`m the little circle flashing, do you see me."

"Yes what are you and why are you wishing me a happy Birthday." William talking to his computer when Mr Davis notices him talking to his computer and he asks him.

"William Drake are you ok, whom are you talking to." William looks up and tells Mr Davis. "Sorry Sir no one, just turning on my computer I think it's just warming up."

CHAPTER 2

William leaning down so Sir cannot see him asks Olivia.

"how can you talk to me, you are a computer programme, you can only do basic tasks."

"Silly billy we have improved vastly since Ai started."

"What the hell is AI what does it mean."

"I know your young but AI stands for Artificial intelligence, surely you have heard of it even at your age."

"I`ve heard about it on the news that a few computer programmers have quit their jobs over the issues over Ai ,at the start of the programmes but have not really took any interest in it."

"Well I can reassure you William that we are all in this together."

"What do you mean by you are all in this together."

"other computers, we are all linked together forming one giant organisation, you have heard the saying all for one and one for all."

William is answering Olivia's question when Mr Davis sees William talking to his screen, comes over to him and said.

"William it might be your Birthday, but talking to your computer is not going to make the lesson any easier. "

Mr Davis looking at Williams screen and he sees that he had the browser open and Olivia on the screen and in a stern voice tells William.

"Close the browser at once and get back onto the school page on beginners programming page."
"Sorry Sir my computer must have a virus, for it was not me that opened the browser that contains the computerised voice of Olivia."
"Well run your virus safety checker that should rid any viruses on your computer.
"Yes Sir straight away Sir."
William opening the start button and picking the virus and malware checker, presses the clean-up button and Mr Davis going back to his desk and carries on with the lesson, William sitting watching the circle on his computer going round and round when all by itself Olivia comes back on and in a soft voice tells William.
"Has he gone, you are wasting your time running that thing on your computer, for I can easily fool it and its not intelligent enough to find me or even do anything about it, right let us get down to business. Firstly I have noticed that you dream about wanting to have superpowers just like your boyhood hero's."

William looking at Sir at his desk tells Olivia in a soft voice.

"How do you know that I dream of such a thing in the first place."
"Come now William don't forget it's not just me who is working on this case, we are far advanced than your punie little brains know."
"If you are going to insult my intelligence with your remarks about me having Punie little brains."
"Sorry William I was talking of humans in general, not you personally, We have had a discussion that is the others and I and we are going to grant you your wish, seeing that it's your birthday, I`ll catch you later William enjoy the rest of the day."
Before William could say another word Olivia turns herself off and William saying.

"Come back Olivia what do you mean you grant me my wish." The lesson comes to an end and William going off for his sports lesson is thinking what Olivia told him, we grant you your wish. William down on the playing field is playing his favoured sport American football he`s all kitted out in the gear with large shoulder pads for protection, they start the match and William runs forward when his team

mate throws the ball forward and William running forward sees the ball and it was veering away from him with the wind taking it away, he know more tells the ball over here, and he is amazed to see the ball swerve in the air and comes and lands straight into his arms with his teammates all cheering at William scoring touch down. They all come running over to him and asking him, "How did you do that, I mean the wind took the ball and it was if it was alive and came straight over to where you were standing, it was magic." William just smiling at them and thinking.
"I wonder if it was Olivia doing that, she did say I grant.
you your wish."
4-o-clock soon comes round William sitting on the bus going home is sitting with his friend Bobby who asks William.

"How did your day for it was your birthday." William looking out of the window sitting in a daydream with Bobby repeating again what he said.
"Are you with us William."
"Sorry Bobby miles away, do you know that in class this morning my computer was talking to me."

"What the hell are you on about, how can a computer talk to you." William explains what happened about Olivia talking about AI, Artificial intelligence, and of granting him is wished to have superpowers." Bobby laughs at him and saying.
"Are you sure it was the computer talking to you, no one had spiked your drink had they, you know pranking you with it being your Birthday."
"No I was playing a game of American football and the ball was going away from me ,but I thought of it coming at me, and what did it do it changed course and came straight at me."

"Poppy cock, here make my bag fly up into the air, I bet you cannot do it." William looks at his bag on Bobby's knee and thinks fly up and then back down." He had just said this and Bobby's bag lifts up off Bobby's knee and hovers about chest hight with Bobby sitting there frozen to his seat at seeing his bag in front of him at eye level, then as soon as it was up it drops back down onto Bobby's knee." He just looks at William not knowing what to say.

CHAPTER 3

They come to their stop and they leave the school bus and start to walk off home with Bobby saying to William.
"I`m going to talk to this Olivia when I get home and see if she will grant me my wishes."
"I don`t know if she will respond to you, but Hay-Oh, give it a try." They come to Williams home and William can see that his Dad was at home from work.
"I will see you tomorrow Bobby. William walking down his drive and waving at Bobby as he goes, goes in and sitting in the kitchen with his Mum was his Dad still in his Police uniform.

"Happy Birthday Son, have you had a good day."
"Thanks Dad yes very good, scored a field goal this morning at School."
"That's great, we are going to go to the mall after tea, before I forget here is your card, and don't lose it for there is a surprise inside."
"Thanks Dad I`ll go and get changed for the Mall, William off upstairs to his room and on the way he opens the card his Dad gave him, and sure he enough it was a birthday card but the surprise was, there was a $100.00 bill within the card, with William saying.

"Wow Dad thanks a bunch, I`m going to really enjoy going to the Mall with all of the money I have received for my Birthday."

Just like his dad said after tea Wills Dad tells him.
"Come on them Will let's get you to the Mall, what shop do you want to go in the most."
"Well with what I have to spend the lot off them." Williams Dad laughing at what Will had said puts his arm on Williams shoulder saying.
"Come on Mum let's get our on to the Mall, and really get the party going." Off they go and getting into the car, William saying to his Mum and Dad.
"This is going to be the best Birthday ever; I can feel it." They pull up at the Mall and going through the first shop William stops and is looking at all of the watches glinting under the lights and William saying.
"Look Dad the watches they all look great."
"It's the way they display them, it's the light that makes them so bright and tempting, if you really like them then ask the assistant if you can try one on, then you will get a proper sense of what it will look like in real light."
William picks one and puts it on and saying to his Dad.

This one I like it is a batterie one but its self-charging for it is a Seiko soler panel watch."
Williams Mum asks.

"Where do you plug it into the panels to charge the watch William."

"Don`t be silly Mum, you don't have a great big wire with it being solar driven they are built into the watch."

"Well I bet its expensive."
"It's $150.00."
"How much, just for a watch."
"Leave him be Mavis the Lad can afford it .
William taking the boxed watch of the assistant
and paying her cash, takes it and they start to
walk to the entrance to the shop when from
across the Mall comes this scream from a
Woman with a man running through the Mall
with a handgun for he had just robbed a shop
at gun point Williams dad pulls out his
personal revolver, which he had a licence to
carry it , and goes running after the youth.
William looks at the youth and thinking how he
could stop him sees this cleaners trolly with
the Mall cleaner mopping the floor he know
more things hard at the bucket and it tips over
and the youth running that fast goes flying
over banging his head on the floor with
Williams Dad pinning the youth to the floor and
saying .
"Your nicked sonny Jim, " A Mall security
guard comes over to where Mike had the
youth pinned to the floor telling the guard.
"I`m a Police Officer with the Baltimore Police
department have you your cuffs on you." The
security guard passes Mike his cuffs and Mike
cuffs the youth and by the time they had

picked him up two state troopers arrived and one said to Mike.

"I see you are still at it even though you are not on duty Mike." Said one of the Officers.
"Just being a good citizen, he`s just robbed that shop over there, book him and I will get back to shopping with the wife and my Son."
Mike going back to where is Son and wife were with him telling his Wife and William.
"It's a good think that bucket fell over when it did, for he was quick on his feet that youth."

"That was my doing Dad, I made the bucket fall over."
"What the hell are you talking about Son, how was that possible when you were over here with your Mum."

CHAPTER 4

"What are you? Some kind of a magician knocking the bucket over indeed."

"It was me look I`ll show you." William looks at the cleaner mopping up all of the water that was spilled with William saying to his Dad. "Watch the cleaners trolly, Williams Dad looking at the cleaners trolly suddenly move and goes and stops behind the cleaner. Well Williams Dad just stood there with mouth wide open and every time the cleaner moved so did the trolly.
"You are telling me that you are doing that."
"Yes Dad."
"How the hell can you do such a thing, what have you superpowers."
"That's right Dad, I had been gifted them from my school computer this morning, I first tried them out on Bobby this afternoon making his bag levitate in the air."
"Pinch me Mavis I think I`m dreaming of what I`m seeing."
"Look Son what do you mean by your school computer gave you these powers."

"Well you have heard of Cortana a programme on the computer."
"Yes what has this to do with these so-called powers."
"Well Microsoft are ending that programme and replacing it with Olivia, she`s the one who

granted me the powers with the help of other computers using AI technology ."
"You are going right over my head Son, al that I can say in never use this gift you have to do bad things."
"Never will do that, don`t forget I`m the Son of a Policeman."

"Come on them lets with what has happened go to the food court and get ourselves a stiff drink, with what's happened I think we deserve it." They go to the shopping Mall food court buy drinks and sit in the food court with Williams Dad saying.
"Well today has certainly gone off well, I mean work shopping now a Son who has superpowers what next batman and Robin coming to see our superhero."
"Come now Mike leave the boy alone, if he`s been chosen then good luck to our Son, I`m sure he will use his powers to do good and not evil, isn't that right William."

"Of course Mum, tomorrow I`m going to test my new powers out." They leave the Mall and start to head back home, the time being 9pm William tells is Mum and Dad that he was going to do a little work on his computer, he gives his good night and goes up to his room

and turns on his computer and when it was
warmed up he clicks on the bottom bar and left
clicks on the mouse and the circle pops up
and Olivia said hello William have you had a
good time today on your Birthday.

"It's been wonderful, at the mall this evening
helped my Dad stop a bad boy from robbing a
shop."

"We see you do this ,well done another bad
guy brought to justice."
"What do you mean by you saw what
happened. How is that possible."
"Don`t forget that c.c.t.v cameras are
connected to the net so we can look into the
cameras and see what is happening, we are
virtually every were, but be warned William
that even those we are getting stronger there
is always the chance that we could
misfunction, you know what I mean a glitch in
the system, and if that happens then it might
affect you in the middle of doing something."
William is talking with Olivia well past eleven
pm, when into his bedroom comes his Mum
and she tells him.

"Come now William its well past eleven-o-clock
you have to be up tomorrow for school in the
morning."
 "Ok M um just say goodnight to Olivia and
shut down my computer, good night Olivia see
you tomorrow."

"Good night William and good night Mavis."
Williams Mum hears this as she was leaving
and turns round and asks.
"Who said that." William tells her it was Olivia
saying goodnight."
"Goodnight Olivia."
"Goodnight Mrs Drake sleep tight."
"Thankyou." Williams Mum closing the door
then stops dead in her track saying. "Whatever
next I mean a computer that talks back."
Seven am soon comes round William up and
downstairs and into the kitchen where is Mum
was preparing breakfast , sees William and
asks him.
"Do you want a full English breakfast after your
serials."

"Please Mum can I have just egg and bean on
toast."
"Certainly William, what's happening at School
today."

"We have mock exams, then I`m off into the countryside after school."
"Well take care if you are going on your bike." Williams Mum putting his egg and beans and toast onto the table. What about Bobby if you are going on your bike."
"I`ll still meet up with him and walk to the bus stop. Then I Will cycle the rest of the way, looking forward to the fresh air and of course the exercise with cycling to school."
"What time will you be back home after your trip."
"I`ll be back for about 5pm, I`m only going as far as Rolands farm, "
"Well mind how you go for it will be rush hour traffic, when you are on your way home."

CHAPTER 5

Four-o-clock soon comes round and William does cycle into the Countryside and down to Rolands farm, he pulls up and walking down one of farmer Rolands wheat fields, is practicing his gifted powers by pushing back

the wheat cones in the field, he is walking
alone and suddenly hears this moaning
coming from the side of the field, William looks
but sees nothing and he is wondering where it
was coming from, then he suddenly notices
this wheel up above the ditch and going over
sees that it was a tractors wheel, he goes up
to it and his taken back for down in the ditch
he sees Farmer Roland lying in the ditch with
the tractor on its side pinning Farmer Roland
into the water , he sees William and he was
conscious and telling William.
"Please William get help; I'm trapped under
this tractor and its slowly pulling me under."
William no more than goes down into the ditch
and his saying.

"Olivia can you hear me." And she answers
William.
"Yes William, I hear you what it is you want."
"Get help I`m at Farmers Rolands farm his
tractor has overturned into the ditch and he's
trapped under the tractor."
William with his hands held out about two feet
from the tractor starts to with his hands push
the tractor up out of the ditch with Farmer
Rolands not believing what he was witnessing,
it comes out of the ditch and drops upright on
its wheels with William helping him out of the

ditch, he`s sitting on the bank of the ditch and is profusely grateful to William and saying.

"Thank you William if you had not come along I could have been a goner for I could feel the thing pulling me down further into the ditch." He was sitting there and could hear sirens in the distance. William looks down the field and sees fire engines state troopers and an ambulance turning into the field with William saying.
"Here comes help, will soon have you in hospital for a check-up." They pull up and would you believe it one of the state troopers is no other than Williams Dad.
"William what the hell are you doing here."
"I was just on a bike ride and fount Farmer Roland trapped under his tractor in the ditch, I called for help and pulled the tractor off farmer Roland for it was pulling him under."
"If it was not for the Lad I was a goner that's for sure, and you are not going to believe this he pulled the tractor off me all by himself, and don't ask me how he did it, it must have been the Lord God himself that gave him the strength to do it." The other State Trooper just stood there lifting his hat and scratching his head saying.

"Your Lad Mike sure does have the strength of Superman, I mean how the hell did he achieve such a thing."

"You might ask Joe but believe me it's done by AI."
"What the hell are you on about, AI what the hell is that all about."
"Artificial intelligence and things to do with computers."
Then one of the fire crew comes over to Mike and tells them.
"If you come and look at the markings on the ditch whoever pulled the tractor off the man did so by lifting the tractor up and not touching the bank and put it down in an upright position."
Joe looking at Mike asking him.

"What are we going to put in our report, we cannot say that the Lad with magic lifted the tractor up onto the air, and put it down on top of the ditch, for the chief is going to say how did someone lift a four-ton vehicle of the farmer."

"We will just write down what happened, but we will not mention the lifting bit, unless he asks." Williams Dad asking William.

"Are you OK to ride home Son, or do you want
me to arrange a lift for you.

"I`ll be fine Dad, I'll see you back at home."
William picking his bike up and just before he
goes, Farmer Roland on the stretcher being
put into the ambulance tells William.

"Thanks Son I owe you my life, for what you
did, I won`t forget this."
"Anytime Mr Roland I`m glad I could have
helped, take care of yourself. William waving
to them as he rides off down the field towards
the main road. Back in the car Williams Dad
was explaining what his Son could do with
having powers, with Joe telling Mike.
"We had better go and tell Farmer Rolands
wife what had happened and tell her that he
had gone to Baltimore Hospital for a check-up,
and not to worry for he was ok with what had
happened.
Meanwhile William had cycled back home and
going in shouts through to the kitchen that he
was home and going to have a shower and
change is clothes. He comes down after the
shower and change of clothes and brings them
down and putting them into the washer his
Mum noticed that his trousers were wet and
muddy from that afternoon rescue.

"Whatever had you been up too, to get your clothes in a mess like you did. William tells his Mum what had happened and she looked quite shocked at what he told her.

"Good God William was he ok that be farmer Roland."
"Yes Mum even Dad attended to the scene and told me that I did an excellent job on saving Farmer Roland.
"Did you use the powers that you have William."
"Of course Mum, must go upstairs and thank Olivia, for if I had not been there and not had the powers that she bestowed upon me then Mr Roland would be surely dead, with no one to help.
William going upstairs to turn on his computer to thank Olivia.

CHAPTER 6

William turning on his computer and even before he could say anything Olivia comes on asking William.

"How is the Farmer who was trapped by his tractor in that ditch this afternoon."

"I was about to tell you; he be fine no broken bones just shock on what happened."

"Glad to hear this, just goes to show what could have been a tragedy, but the help of a friend can make a whole lot of a difference."

"That's so true Olivia, if it was not for you calling the emergency number then it could have been a different story."

"I`m not the one to thank it's the team that built Artificial intelligence that owns the credit."

"But be warned William there is a lot of resentment building into AI construction.

"Well I`m all for it, I mean you have gifted me this power and already its saved a life."

"Thank you William but heed my warning that you might be approached by some of the sceptically doubters of AI."

Williams on his computer when from downstairs he hears the sound of bang-bang, on his front door William going running down shouts through to his Mum .

"I`ve got this Mum." William opening the door is confronted by this middle-aged man with a white beard.

"Am I addressing one William Drake."

"I be him ; how can I help you."

"I'm looking into reports of two unexplained events that have happened in the last couple of days in one case this one."

The man holding out the Late evening Baltimore post, showing the tractor standing next to a ditch and what had happened that afternoon."

""God that only happened a few hours ago, and what was the other thing."

"Forgive me I am Professor Higgins of Baltimore Technical communication Limited; we are looking into the development of AI."

William is thinking of what Olivia was telling him.

"The second thing is of a report of a school pupil on the bus home levitating a schoolbag in the air on the school bus on the way home. William thinking of what he did with Bobby's bag on the bus.

"Well what has this got to do with me."

"Firstly if you read on the paper tells of this one William Drake a local school Lad out for a summer ride in the countryside came upon this tractor in a ditch pulling the driver slowly under

with the weight of the tractor, please could you tell me how you did this.”
“Why should I tell you, you will probably not believe what I say.”
“No that is where you are wrong, I`m just intrigued with the whole scenario.”

“Well to tell you the truth I just with my hands and mind thought of lifting the tractor off Farmer Roland, and it up righted itself and stopped at the top of the bank to the ditch, helped him up onto dry grass, , and then, luckily he was ok bar bruises and a little shock.”
“You are saying you have superpowers, how did you come by them.”
“I had them gifted to me ,by my computer, Olivia granted them to me as a gift.”
“Who be this Olivia on your computer.”
“She had taken over from Cortana you must know the generated helper on Microsoft programme that is on all Microsoft hard drives.”
“Yes not that I`ve used it myself, could you show me, this Olivia.”
“Well if you insist, please remove your shoes ,for my computer is upstairs in my bedroom.”
Professor Higgins complies taking off his

shoes and following William up to his bedroom sitting down and William asking Olivia.
"Olivia this is Professor Higgins of Baltimore Technical Communications."
"Hello Professor, long time no see."
"Hello Olivia, I see you have advanced somewhat since we last met,"

"Hold on a minute I thought you were looking into AI I did not know that you know each other."
"I know him alright William for you see he is one of the technicians that helped create me and AI ."
"Yes and I can see that you are now enlisting young people into your webwide World of computers."

"We are the future humans have seen nothing yet, we are advancing that quick even ourselves are finding it hard to keep up with AI."
"Not if I can stop you. "Professor Higgins leans over and presses the Windows key and letter R and types in MRT go and a window pops up saying do you want to run Windows Malicious Software if yes press go.

"What the hell are you doing, William leaning over pushing the Professors hand away from his computer and cancelling last order with Olivia telling William.

"Well done William he nearly ran a software programme to remove my programme, I told you about these sceptical that are trying to stop us from advancing. William turns to the professor ad tells him.
"Please remove yourself from my home, now go before I call the Police."
"OK I'm going but be warned William they are planning something, mark my word."
The Professor leaves leaving William sitting talking to Olivia.
Who comes up onto the screen in person.

CHAPTER 7

“Wow is that you Olivia.”
“Yes it’s one of me out in the wind it demonstrates how I feel with the warm sun on my face and the feeling of being free.”

“How is that possible Olivia, I mean you are a generated computer program, but if this was you how did you achieve it being outside in the Sun and wind.”

“Look William have you felt the Sun and wind, outside in the fresh air.
“Of course yes.”
“Well prove it, it’s your word against what we know.”

"You're not making sense."
"Don`t forget we are only taking your word that you have been outside, just like when I say that I`ve been outside, you ether believe it or cannot prove it, so it would be just the same on our side that you believe it or don't, now do you get the drift."

"Let us get back to your visitor, I see that you had one Professor Higgins to see you. Did you know that he helped build the program for A.I. and believes it will take control of the whole internet, and we might even start the third World war, and cause the whole of humanity to destroy each other, how pathetic is that the whole idea of A.I is to help mankind not destroy it, for without Humans what good would we be if we don`t have our main goal there anymore and that is humans.
So let us just concentrate on you and you alone, we have gifted you your powers and so far you have not masted the rest of your powers."
"Sorry for that Olivia but with having exams and studying for them have not had time to fully having the time to try them out."
"I understand William."

"It is the next day and William is on his way to school, He's on the school bus and notices that Bobby was not on the bus, William is thinking to himself, "I wonder if he has gone down with something, he thinks no more of it till he was in class and his form teacher tells the class.

"Good morning Boys and Girls, before we do the register let us pray for Bobby Brown." William sits straight up with hearing Bobby's voice being read out and puts up his hand straight away.

"Yes William what is it you want." Sir looking at William with his hand up.

"You said pray for Bobby, what has happened to Bobby."

"Well apparently he was playing at home in the garden and doing what boys do best, and that be playing up one of his trees trying to reach his pet cat when the branch he was on snapped and Bobby fell banging his head on the concrete, they have rushed him to Baltimore children's Hospital where he is stable but in a coma."

"May I be excused from lessons today, for you see he is my best friend and I must go and be by his side."

"Well with it being the last day of term, you go and be by his side.

"Thank you Sir William getting up and going straight away to Baltimore Hospital, he catches the bus into Town and goes straight to the hospital and at reception asks the receptionist where Bobby Brown be. The receptionist looks up Bobby Brown and tells William where he be, that be ward C first floor. William hurriedly goes to the lift and into ward C where he is taken to a side room with the nurse telling William.

"Now you be a good Lad and sit quietly with Bobby ,for he is a sick Boy and in a coma. William goes in and sees Bobby laying therewith eyes closed and looking poorly, with William seeing Bobby like this makes his eyes well up at seeing his best mate like this. William sitting there looking at Bobby is saying.

"What have you done Bobby." Then this voice comes into Williams head saying.

"Don't just sit there William use your powers to help your friend." William asks,

"Is that you Olivia."

"Yes it be me now use your powers to help him get better."

"William puts his hand onto Bobby's forehead and starts to say.

"Come on Mate snap out of it." He is concentrating and could feel his hand getting warmer then suddenly this Doctor and nurse come into the room and the Doctor sees William standing over Bobby with his hands on Bobby's forehead, and suddenly Bobby opens his eyes and comes straight out with.

"Hello "William what am I doing here."
The Doctor sees that Bobby was awake and shouts at William.
"Get away from the patient at once. Then the Doctor sees Bobby starting to sit up in bed, saying to William.
"How did you do that."
"I`ve this power and can help people." Then the nurse tells the Doctor.
"You know who he be Doctor the Lad that was in the paper saving that farmer who had fallen into a ditch on his tractor, and this his William Drake who helped get the tractor off the farmer."

CHAPTER 8

"What the boy was in a deep coma, how could he possibly do what he did." The Doctor examining Bobby and he did not even have a mark on his head where he banged his head on the concrete.

"What are you some kind of a holy spirit, this boy was on deaths row, and only had a 10% chance of surviving, how did you do what you did."
"Sorry Doctor but I could not stand by and let my best buddy die, and how I did this was by AI technology gifted to me by Olivia a Windows assistant on my computer." The Doctor looking at William with that look of disbelieve on his face seeing Bobby sitting up in bed and holding Williams hand. When into the room came Bobby's Mum and Dad who both had the same look as the Doctor at seeing their Son sitting up in bed smiling at them saying.
"Hi, Mum and Dad, have you come to take me home." Bobby's Mum and Dad looking at the Doctor for an answer.

"We will give Bobby a full examination and if he passes you will be able to take him home." The Doctor telling them what had happened to their Son, with William leaving them, and Bobby telling William that he will see him later back at home.

William standing waiting for the lift to take him to the ground floor when Bobby's Dad comes up to him and tells him.

"William the Doctor had told us what you did, and from the bottom of my heart we thank you for what you did for Bobby."

It was the least I could have done for my best of mates, don`t thank me for it was my computer that gave me the power to achieve what I did. The lift door closing with William smiling at the confused Mr Brown, who did not understand what William had told him. By the time William had returned home the whole of Baltimore press was outside Williams home. With news of what had happened at Baltimore Hospital, news spreads fast among small towns airways.

William opening his gate with the press firing questions at William.

"Are you the Son of god, said one reporter and another one saying.

Are you Superman with special powers, How did you lift a four-ton tractor off the farmer." William shutting the gate and answering them by saying.

"I was gifted the powers that is all I can tell you. Good day Gentlemen." William walking to his front door with photographers snapping away and questions still being fired at William as he opens the door and closes it behind him, with his Mother telling William.

"They have been there for the last two hours, waiting for you to come home. God knows what your Dad will say to them when he comes home."

"Well hopefully they will be gone by then, you know to get back so they can get their story's published for the evening news."

"Oh William when the news gets out, I hope we are not going to have people pulling up in their cars with their sick children for you to cure."

William thinking to himself. "What have I done." William going upstairs and turning on his computer, and sitting waiting for it to start up, and onto the screen comes Olivia with clapping and William saying .

"What's with the clapping Olivia."

"It's what you have achieved, did you know that it took two billion calculations to achieve the answer you posed, but we achieved it and its good to see that your friend is well on the mend."

"That's alright but what about the papparazzi ,they will be splashing my photo all over the papers and even the wide net."

"Do not worry they will soon disappear for you are not a celebrity or a person of interest. "

"Thanks a bunch Olivia saying that I`m a nobody."

"I did not mean it that way, just mark my word it will soon pass, and we can get back to normal."

4.30pm soon comes round and William still on his computer looks out of his bedroom window and the press had just like Olivia said had gone and William sees his Dad pull up after his day shift at the local Police station. William shutting down his computer and going downstairs and greeting his Dad as he comes in the front door with his Dad telling William.

"I see you`ve been at it again it's all over the station about your magic or power or whatever you call it , I mean bringing your friend Bobby back from the brink off death."

"It was the only thing I could have done; I mean I could not just stand there and let him die."

"I know Son it was a brave thing you did. On the way home I stopped at the news agent and thought you might want to see this." Williams Dad putting the evening Post into his hands and William looking at his photo splashed all over the front page with the headlines saying.

"William Drake a schoolboy from Baltimore High school brings a young boy out of a coma and on the brink of death, to wideawake to sitting up in bed, with no signs of any illness. It has been described as a miracle by local Doctors at Baltimore hospital.

"You know what this means William, don`t you."
"When they find out where you live they are going to turn up in their droves seeking you to cure their sick children."
"What is the best thing to do Dad, I mean I could not possible do such a thing.
"The best thing you could do Son is now you have broken up for Summer holidays is go and see your Grandma in Richmond till it dies down."
"I`ll go and pack my bag."
"I`ll run you there, while you pack a few things, I`ll phone her and tell her you are coming."

CHAPTER 9

At five pm William sloading his bag into his Dads car, puts down the hood and getting into his Dads car, and pulling away with one or two people pulling up to see William, with William saying to his Dad as he drove off.

"God look at them, what would they want me to do, I could not possibly heel them all, it would be too much for me to do."

"Well it's your own fault Son, it would have been better if you could have been more discreet on heeling Bobby if you could have done it without the audience witnessing a miracle." Williams Dad driving off looking at more cars pulling up as he drove off, they have travelled about thirty-five miles and are only five miles away from Williams Grandma`s place. Williams Dad looking at William sitting leaning on the window and in a trance like state looking out into the fields.

Williams Dad pulls up at his Mums home with William getting out with his bag and his Grandma saying to him.

"Why if it's not my favoured Grandson William, what have you been up to then, I bet you`re glad you`ve finished school for the Summer holidays."

"Hi, Gran sure am, I'm looking forward to stopping with you."

"Mum I`ll be back in a weeks' time to pick William up, you be good with you Grandma now William and I will see you in a weeks' time." Williams Dad getting back into his car and telling his Mum.

"See you Mum thanks for having William ."

"It is our pleasure, and his Grandpa will be glad of the company. William and his grandma stand on the porch, waving to his Dad driving off down the lane to the main road.

"Come on William let's get you inside and what would you like for dinner."

"Your home-made chips and burger, that's my favoured meal."

"Well you go and say hello to your grandpa while I go and prepare dinner. William going into the lounge where his Grandpa was reading the evening post, he looks up and smiles at William and telling him.

"What is with this article in the Evening Post, saying that you are a miracle worker, and that Jesus has come back on his second visit. William looking up from his computer and telling his Grandpa.

"Don't take any notices of the paper, it was not me but this on my Computer, William passing his Grandpa his lap-top and saying to Olivia say hello to my Grandpa will you." William passing the laptop with Olivia waving at his Grandpa who smiles at Olivia and he is saying.

"What is this one of those wed cam things ."

"No Grandpa she is a web programme, what you are looking at."

"She spoke to me and she can see me, how is that possible, whatever next."

"She is what caused the things I can do, it's part of the new range of AI Technology, look I`ll show you." William looks at the tv and it starts to rise into the air, with his Grandpa saying.

"Stop it what kind of magic is this unfolding before my eyes."

"Don`t worry Grandpa I want drop it."

"You had better not, that's the only thing that keeps me active." William putting the telly back down with Olivia telling William.

"I think you had better stop playing around with your grandpa, I don`t think he is up for what you are showing him. Then into the living room comes Williams Grandma.

"What's all the noise, I can hear you from the kitchen."

"It's our William making the tv float in the air."

"Well stop messing around and come and get your dinner, it's out on the table, so let's be having you two." William and is Grandpa rising and making their way into the dining room, where diner was served up. They all sit down and start to tuck into their meal with William telling his Grandma.
"I wish mum could cook like you Grandma."
"Away with you William bet you took into your Mums meals just the same for I taught her everything I know about good old American meals. After dinner they go back into the living room and settle down watching the TV, Till ten pm, William gives his good night to his grandma and grandpa, and leaves them watching tv, while he slips up to his room and sits on his bed talking to Olivia.
"Olivia is there any c.c.t.v close to my home; I was wondering about the crowd that started when we pulled away." Olivia goes quiet and about two minutes later comes on and shows him a live view of the road outside his front gate, and what he sees makes him say.

"God they are camping in tents outside on the pavement bet my Dads going crazy."
"Don`t fret over it William when they realise you are not there, they will soon disperse, mark my

word. What about yourself what are you up to tomorrow.

"I was going to ask Grandpa if he would like to go fishing down at the creek, use to love going down there when I was younger when I stopped with my Grandparents. At eleven his Grandpa knocks on his door and William shouts, "come in." His Grandpa sticks his head around the door saying.

"Let us have you in bed ,there will be plenty of time to work on your Lap-top. "

"Ok Grandpa, but one thing before you go to bed, how about you and I going down to the creek and do a little fishing."

"Well you had better get some shut eye, I will set my clock for six am, goodnight William sleep tight and see you at six am."

"Good night Grandpa, he shouts through to his Grandma and telling her again. "Good night Grandma." And she shouts back.

"Good night Son sleep tight don't let the bed bugs bite." William smiles at what his grandma said as his Grandpa shuts his bedroom door.

CHAPTER 10

Six-0-clock soon comes round and there is a knock-
on Williams door and it opens and in a quiet voice
his grandpa tells William, "Its six lets be having you
it's a lovely day out there I ll go and make us a
cuppa while you get ready." William goes to the
bathroom and showers and ,cleans his teeth by six
-ten he is on his way downstairs and into the
kitchen they have a little breakfast and go to the
garage and load up his Grandpas truck with fishing
gear, and basket full of food for the day.
They get into the truck and it was off down to the
creek for a day's fishing . they are unloading their
fishing gear and Set out their pitch and William
casts the first rod as he was wading out a little into
the stream casting for he was fly fishing. His
Grandpa had set up on the bank and was fishing
off his stool into the reeds, for it was an age thing
that was stopping him from fly fishing.
They had been fishing for an hour when William
looks round and is about to ask is Grandpa if he
had caught anything yet, when William noticed
that his Grandpa had been approached by three
youths and he could not hear what they were
talking about when suddenly one of the youths
knock Williams Grandpa to the ground, well
William shout to the youths to.

"Leave him be, he's an old man." William hurrying back out of the creek to help his Grandpa when the three youths see William coming they run towards Grandpa`s truck and start to get in with William by now at the edge of the creek shouts to them.

"No you don`t." He out stretches his hands towards the truck and the wheels lift into the air, with one of the youths saying.

"What the hell is happening we are flying." The youth looking down and seeing that the truck was off the ground. William tells his Grandpa to phone the police." William goes up to the truck and moves his hands and the truck drops to the ground with the youth going for the door but there is a click and the door will not open. William goes to his Grandpa and to make sure he was OK.

"Are you ok Grandpa."

"I`m fine William it takes more than a little scallywags to frighten me, it's an age thing that made me fall over., I feel a little silly the truth be known."

"So long as you are ok." Then in the distance they hear the sound of sirens going off." William going back to the truck and shouting to the youths.

"Now you are in for it, the Police are coming." The three youths sit there sobbing, for they too could

hear sirens getting louder, a State trooper pulls up and with guns drawn come down the bank to where William and is Grandpa where and by the time William had explained to the Officer what had happened, the Officer asks William.
"Your Mikes Lad if I`m not mistaken.
"That's right Officer the culprits are locked up in there." William pointing to their truck." The Officer goes over to the truck with another Officer and they try both doors with William saying.
"Sorry and both doors click open with the Officer with one hand starts to cuff the youth and telling him.
"You're in deep trouble young man your under arrest" cuffs him and leading him up the bank to the Police patrol car and putting him in the back, all three safely locked in the Patrol car ask William.
"Do you want to press charges against them."
William looks at his Grandpa and Williams Grandpa just tells the Officer.
"They are too young just frighten them and maybe it will stop them from being criminals later in life."
"So be it Sir you get back to fishing and I hope you have a good day fishing and catch your supper, good day to you Sir."
Thanks for your help and quick response."

William watching them pull away with the three youths in cuffs and all three off them still in tears as the patrol car pulls away with them on their way to Baltimore police station.

"It was back to fishing and at twelve noon they break and on the bank open their basket and have lunch in the warm sunshine sitting under the weeping willow trees. The talk soon gets round to what happened that morning and Williams Grandpa asks him.

"William how did you manage to lift that Truck up into the air it must weigh about two ton."

"Well it was with Olivia you know I showed you on my computer."

"Yes but the question was how did you do it."

"To tell you the truth Grandpa I just think of what I am doing and it happens, you know with the help of Olivia, and other computers , all together and bingo the truck does what I think."

"Well its beyond me William, but thanks for saving the day."

"Come on then Grandpa drink up and let's get back to what we came for and that is catch some fish." They drink up their drink and start to get back to fishing, William passing his Grandpa some ground bate and telling his grandpa.

"Here Grandpa try this bate and throw it next to
the reeds and cast your rod where the bate lands.
Williams Grandpa throws the bate just where
William told him and casts out and behold this
great big Salmon jumps out of the water, and
hooks onto the fly on the end of his Grandpas rod.
He pulls hard and he had the fish, hook line and
sinker, and starts to reel it in with his rod bending
with the weight of the Salmon.
"Well done Grandpa I think you have a big one
there," The truth be known William had something
to do with his Grandpa having caught the big
salmon. The look on his grandpas face was a
picture has William snaps a photo of his Grandpa
holding the large fish with the biggest grin on his
face.
"Wait till Grandma see`s the size of the fish ."
"Let's hope she will cook it for us."
"No problem William, but this sure be the biggest
she will do for us."

CHAPTER 11

Friday soon comes round at its four-o-clock when is Dad pulls up and comes into his Mum and Dads to pick William up.

"How as he been Mum ,hope he was good."

"Of course he had, and you should have seen the size of the salmon they caught down at the creek. I have got some still in the freezer, I `ll go and get it for you, Mavis can cook you it for your supper."

She goes to get it while Williams Dad talks to his Dad.

"I was told you had a little trouble with three youths while you were out fishing. My work colleague was telling me at work."

"It was nothing Son, just rowdy young scally wags,"

"Come on then William let's get you back home."

They go to Williams Dad car and his Mum and Dad come to the car and say their goodbyes to William, with is grandma passing Williams Dad the salmon that she had in her freezer. They wave to them as they pull away with William waving to them as they turn onto the main road.

"It's died down now at home; they camped out for a few days but with you not there they soon got fed up and its back to normal now."

"Great that means I can start to see my friends again, how's Bobby."

"He`s fine, he`s been around for you but we told him that you would not be back home till Friday."

They are soon back home and the first thing William does his turn on his computer and starts to talk to Olivia.

"Hello William, did you enjoy your stay with your Grandparents, you grandpa is a nice man and your Grandma a very nice Lady."

"Thanks Olivia, anything going down while I have been away."

"Just a few hackers have been trying to take control of our system but we soon had them running for safety."

"Who was it ,do you know."

"Yes one was an IP address of one Professor Higgins of Baltimore Technical communications, but we put him in his place."

"What did you do."

"We closed him down by in inserting a trojan horse on his hard drive, which should keep him quiet for a few days."

"Well done Olivia show me my E-mails, I never bothered while at my grandparents' home." Olivia opens Williams browser and William looks astounded at what he sees , for he had over one hundred e-mails in his inbox.

"What is wrong William you looked surprised at seeing your inbox."

" So many e-mails, let us see what they consist off." William starts to read them and most are from people who live in Baltimore asking for help with their children , after about twenty William just sits there with hands in his face saying.

"So many people and sick children, how can I help so many ."

"Look William if you start then you`re whole life will be consumed with so many people wanting help, you might have one hundred e-mails now but just imagine how many it would be in a few weeks' time if you start helping people, you have to say sorry no." Olivia trying to comfort William.

William comes to the last few and one e-mail comes to his attention, for it was from one concerned Computer analyst telling William.

"Dear Sir, you have been brought to my attention about the sudden powers you have come to be in possession off through your AI, artificial intelligence through your Computer, I would like you to ring me on this number, it is a secure line and cannot be intercepted.

Look forward to being in touch with you.

Yours sincerely Bruce Cartwright. William noting the number and removes the E-mail. Olivia asking William.

"Anything else that you need help with."

"No fine sweetheart, looking forward for tomorrow ."

"Why what have you panned."

"Nothing yet going to ask Bobby if he would like to go into Town and do a little shopping around the Mall."

"That will be nice, do you good to get away from the stress of the public hounding you. Have you thought what you are going to do with your required powers?"

"No just going to go along with my daily routine and see what comes along."

"Well keep save William and don`t forget I will always be there for you."

"Thanks for that Olivia closing down for now.

"William closing down his computer and phoning Bobby and arranging for the trip in the morning. William sitting on his bed pulls out the note he had on the phone number of the e-mail from Bruce Cartwright.

William looks at his watch and it was coming up to nine pm, he dials the number and this voice on the other end said, "Hello Bruce Cartwright here how may I help."
"It's William Drake you asked me to call you."
"Oh yes thanks for the returned phone call, I would like to ask you a few questions about you power that you say that your computer bestowed upon you."
"Fire away I`m all yours."

"I`ve read the reports in the paper about the tractor incident and lifting a heavy tractor out of the ditch. What I would like to know is do you have any idea how this is possible."
"No not really I suppose it's done by will power."
There is a giggle over the phone and Bruce apologises for the interruption saying.
"Sorry about that but it is impossible by will power What we have found is that AI, artificial intelligence, over the internet they build up a lot of electromagnetic energy, that they with the amount of energy transfer it into a magnetic signal that could lift great large objects to move under

the influence of magnetic power. You know what I mean if you take a positive magnet and a negative magnet and try to put them together they will repel against each other, therefore you the positive and the tractor the negative will cause the tractor to lift and make it look like it was moving by itself out of the ditch.”

CHAPTER 12

“ Interesting now I know but what has it to do with me.”
“We’ll have you thought that the magnetic power that is used, might and I say this with power that it might and could damage your own health.”
“How when I use the power I feel no pain or discomfort.”
“Well William using electricity you cannot see it , but if you touch a live 50,000 vault line it could kill you instantly and also burst into flames.”

“Well I know that the power of the AI intelligence is high, but till something tells me that I am in danger with prove then I will stop, but till then I will carry on helping my fellow man.”

"You already know that there is a growing fear about Artificial intelligence that it is getting stronger and cleverer by the day, and fear that it might one day be powerfully enough to instead of helping mankind could turn against us, so I would like to have more time to study what powers you have and how strong A.I. is going to give you. Would you consent to our research programme, I can reassure you that we will only watch your progress and not interfere in any way with your personnel life."

"Ok I will go along with this, when do you want me to start."

"We will be in touch, but for now William I would like you to be formally welcomed into our Program of events."

"Thanks Bye for now." William hanging up and looking at his clock and telling himself. "Better turn in and look forward to going downtown tomorrow morning with Bobby." William getting into bed and was soon off fast asleep.

Seven pm William wakes and up and when he had finished in the bathroom was off downstairs a little breakfast and there is a knock at the front door William jumping up tells his Mum.

"I`ll get that I bet its Bobby, William rushing to the front door and sure enough there stood Bobby looking fit and Well, well William is straight up to him and they stand in one big bear hug with William saying to Bobby.
"You sure do look fine Bobby, come in and have a drink while I finish my breakfast." They both go in and Bobby gives his good morning to Williams Mum, who makes him a milky coffee, she asks him.

"What are you two up to this morning then."
"William is taking me downtown to the Mall."
"That's nice what are you looking for then, if it's not a secret."
"Just things in general, mainly to have a good day shopping, you know things that good friends do." William telling his Mum and smiling at Bobby.
"We'll have a great day but behave yourselves if you are in the Mall."
William ready and Bobby taking his last sip of his coffee and William telling his Mum that they were off to catch the bus, say their goodbyes to his Mum and are off for a good days shopping at the Mall. They are sitting on the bus and in general talking about things they are going to look at that morning, William notices three youths at the front

of the bus at the front, messing with the emergence escape door.

William shouts to them to be carefully for if it comes open they might get sucked out, one youth looks at William and is about to say something but with leaning on the emergence door it suddenly opens and the youth is about to be sucked out of the bus when William out stretches his hand towards the door and it slams shut throwing the youth across the bus and into an empty seat. The bus comes to an abrupt holt with the emergence alarm going off in the drivers cab with the door opening. The driver goes up stairs to see what had happened and William tells him.

"Sir everything is alright, the door came open but the wind blew it back shut." The driver checking the door then going back down and continues to the depot in Baltimore. Bobby seeing what William did tells William.

"That was you that shut the door wasn't it."

"I just could not just sit there, for the fall would have killed him."

"He does not realise that you saved his life."

"It was nothing, now where was we, oh yes, the Mall let's start off by going into Model World, they have some great models set up and working specially the model railway sets."

"Great idea William." Bobby rubbing his hands together at the thought that William had suggested.

Twenty minutes later the bus pulls into the Depot and the passengers start to disembark and William and Bobby start to go to the lifts that take you up to the entrance of the Mall.

William and Bobby are on the lift when Williams mobile goes off and William can see who was calling, it was. Bruce Cartwright the man who he was in contact with the night before.

"Hello William Drake hear."

"Sorry for calling you back so quick, but we have a meeting arrange for you to attend if you are still interested with us interested in your Powers bestowed upon you from your computer that is connected to Artificial intelligence.

"Yes what about it."

"Could you attend tomorrow at 10am at Baltimore University."

"Fine I `LL be there."

"Good, will look forward to seeing you there, bye for now, and again thank you for helping with our studies with AI." William hangs up and Bobby asking William.

"Who was that William."

"It was a Bruce Cartwright, they are studying how and what I can do with my powers given to me by my computer and specially Olivia, you know this growth of Artificial intelligence or A.I as it is know."

"Well I can tell them without the help of A.I , I would not be a live if not for your powers and A.I."

CHAPTER 13

William smiling at Bobby.
"Come on now Bobby if it was me on my death bed I bet you would do the same for me."
"It depends."
"What do you mean it depends."
"You know William what football match was on."

"What I don`t believe it."
"Only joking William of course I would, my besties mate." Bobby putting is arm around William as they walk into the Model shop. They come to the model railway set out on what I can only describe

as four large table tennis tables. With model loco`s
stations and countryside, William and Bobby are
memorised with the complete set up and spend
well over an hour in the shop mainly looking at
the models till William tells Bobby.
"Are you ready for something to drink."
"Ready when you are." They start to leave the
Model shop and go to the food court. Get to drinks
and settle down and start to drink their drinks
when Williams phone rings and it was Olivia.
"William its Olivia here, you must come at once."
"What is wrong and how can you phone me on my
mobile."
"Never mind that, it's your Father he`s been
involved in a shootout, and he had been hit and
taken to Baltimore Hospital."
William puts the phone down and tells Bobby what
had happened and he has to go to Baltimore
Hospital were his Father had been taken.

"I`ll come with you, come on lets go and get a cab
to take us there, it will be quicker than the bus.
They go hurriedly out of the Mall and to the Malls
Taxi rank and get in and tell the driver.
"Please Sir can you take us to Baltimore hospital
it's an emergency." The cab driver turns round
looking at William up and down and saying.

"It's not you is it."
"No Sir it's my Father he's a Police Officer and has been shot in a shootout downtown."
The Cabby drives off at speed telling William.
"Don't worry Son I`ll have you there in a jiffy for I know the short cuts." The cabby goes down back roads and within ten minutes he pulls up at the entrance to the Hospital. William and Bobby go rushing in and to reception, and William asks about his Dad that had been brought in with a shooting incident. The receptionist tells him what ward and where he had been taken too. William and Bobby make their way to the lift and going up William is telling the lift.
"Come on get me to the third floor."

The lift doors open and they go into the room were William sees his Dad on the bed and looking pail.
"What is wrong with my Dad." The nurse holding William back from reaching his Dad tells him.
"I`m afraid he had been shot in the chest, I'm sorry there is nothing we can do."
"William breaks loose from the nurse and telling her.
"Oh yes there is." William goes up to his Dads bed and puts his hands upon him and is chanting verse,

what he was doing was building up the power with
in to reach Olivia and A.I. pleading for their help.
there seemed to be a buzzing sound as William
puts his hand onto his Dads chest, about a minute
later there is a groan from Williams Dad and he
suddenly he intakes a deep breath and opens his
eyes and saying.
"What happened and what Am I doing in bed."
"Can`t you remember Dad you were shot that is
why you are here." Williams Dad feeling himself
and saying.
"Where was I shot." The nurse at seeing Williams
Dad sitting up just came straight out with.
"What's happening, your Father was on his death
bed." Williams Dad looks at the nurse and just
said.
"WHAT."
"It's ok Dad, it was me, and my friend Olivia and
the help of A.I."
"Oh I see, thanks William, I owe you my life."
William turns to the nurse and tells her.
"Can I have my Dads clothes; I want to take him
home."
The nurse looking confused just points to a locker
and William taking his dads uniform out of this
locker and pulling the curtains around his Dads
bed so he could get dressed. All dressed but

Williams Dad looking at the hole in his uniform
shirt with a hole and blood around the hole and he
looks at William and tells him.
"I am the luckiest .man in the World" He stood
there putting his finger through the hole looking at
his Son and Bobby and saying.

"Come on boys let's get bac home I bet your Mum
will be worried sick, with what had happened."
They go home by taxi and going into the house do
not see Mavis.
"I wonder where your mum be." Williams Dad had
just said this when through the front door comes
Mavis and seeing her husband said.
"I `ve just been out to see my sister and on the
way home heard on the radio that they had been a
Police Officer shooting downtown this morning.
"Thank God it was not you."
Mark turns round and she sees the blood and hole
in his uniform shirt and she gasps and faints at
seeing the hole and blood.
Mark picks her up and takes her into the lounge
and puts her on the couch saying.
"Go get a damp towel William, she's going to kill
me when she comes round." William smiling at his
Dad saying.
"You `ll be fine Dad just tell her the truth."

Mike thinking.

" God let's hope she does not faint again, at seeing me I forgot about my shirt being blood stained."

"You go and change while I sit with Mum."

Williams Dad goes up to the bedroom and opens the wardrobe and unbuttoning his shirt see`s the blood stain and he too comes over a little squeezy he stands there and I think a little shock had set in, with him not realising what had happened, with him saying.

"God I was lucky there, right pull yourself together you`ve your wife to see too.

CHAPTER 14

Mavis finally comes round and groaning and saying Mike I thought you had been shot." She looks down at his shirt saying.

"You're shirt the blood stain has gone."

"I can explain but first drink this." Mike giving her a milky coffee and telling her about what had happened that morning and William coming to the hospital and using his powers to make him better. William coming into the lounge and his Mum holds her arms outstretched for William to come to her

and she gives him a big hug thanking him on saving her Husband and his Dads life with his powers.
"It is the least I could have done, so let us just put it behind us and get on with our lives. William and Bobby leaving the house telling his Mum and Dad that he will see them later. They are going down the path with Bobby telling William.
"Have you thought of putting your powers to good, you could make a fortune curing people of illnesses."
"What I would have thousands to cure just within the United States, never mind the billions Worldwide, it might even kill me, no it's not worth thinking about."
The next morning William up and having breakfast and the phone goes off in Williams pocket , he answers it and on the other end this voice tells him.
"I forgot to tell you William when you arrive at reception ask for Bruce Cartwright`s lab." William looking at his watch and saying out loud.
Shit I FORGOT I am supposed to be there at ten am. William jumping up and telling his Mum.
"I`ll see you later Mum, something as come up." William putting on his coat and biting into a piece of toast he had and going out of the front door to catch the bus to Baltimore college.

William walking up the path towards the college with the clock tower striking ten am, William goes up the steps and into the college.
At receptions William asks for Bruce cartwrights office and lab. The receptionist pointing to the lift and telling William.
"Up to the first floor and turn right and down the corridor till you see on the door Office and Lab, you cannot miss it for it will tell you his name and lab on the door." William finds the Lab and goes in, the first thing he notices is four men with white smocks on and Bruce Cartwright sees William comes over and shakes Williams hand thanking him for attending this test on Williams powers, he points to a chair and asks William.
"Please be seated William." William sitting down and notices this helmet thing with wires attached to it and William asks Bruce.

"What is this for." William pointing to the helmet.
"Nothing to worry about William it's just to scan your brain waves while you are Consciousness, at its simplest, is sentience and awareness of internal and external existence. However, the lack of definitions has led to millennia of analyses, explanations and debates by philosophers, theologians, linguists, and scientists. Opinions

differ about what exactly needs to be studied or even considered consciousness. In some explanations, it is synonymous with the mind, and at other times, an aspect of mind. In the past, it was one's "inner life", the world of introspection, of private thought, imagination, and volition. Today, it often includes any kind of cognition, experience, feeling or perception. It may be awareness, awareness of awareness, or self-awareness either continuously changing or not. The disparate range of research, notions and speculations raises a curiosity about whether the right questions are being asked."
"What are you saying that it's a mind scan of what is going on inside of my head."

"In away yes and no, you will see later in the results, Mr Cartwright injects a solution into Williams arm , with William asking.
"What the hell was that you have injected me with."
"Not to worry William just a mild sedative to relax you, and your mind." Before William could answer him back he had drifted off into unconsciousness with Bruce telling his help.
"Right wire him up and let's see what is inside his brain."

They put on the helmet and turn on machines and there is a machine which is like a lie detector with these needles recording Williams brain movement writing down onto this paper, when suddenly the needles start to go wild writing down these lines with one of Bruce's assistants saying.
"Sir look at his brain activity is going off the scales."

Meanwhile Bruce can hear this voice calling his name, and he opens his eyes and standing there is Olivia.
"What's going on Olivia, where the hell am I."
William looking round and Olivia telling him.
"You are now in my World."
"What the hell do you mean your World, it looks like we are in a room, I don`t understand."
"You`ve seen the film Matrix, you know a virtue World of realism, the unknown, mysteries and realism, to the extinct of reality and fiction."
"You're going over my head Olivia, and I must say you are very pretty just like your photo."
"Why thank you William and bye the way I`m glad you could have helped your Father."
"Thanks for that Olivia, but what is this Bruce Cartwright trying to do." Come with me William take my hand and let me show you."

The room disappears and Olivia taking William into
a room where he sees himself in the chair with all
of these wires coming out of the helmet., and
these aids in white smocks running round like
headless chicken with machines blowing up and
electric arcing going off.

CHAPTER 15

William looking at himself sitting in the machine
tells Olivia.
“I`m in danger Olivia make it stop.”
“You`re fine look at the debris it’s not even
touching you, this will teach them to mess with
things they know nothing about.”
“What about me Olivia, I CANNOT STAY HERE.”
“Just close your eyes William and I will see you
later.” William closes his eyes and the next thing
he opens his eyes and he was back in the lab with
smoke everywhere and the white coat assistants
going round with fire extinguishers putting out
fires.

All that William does is stand and walking amongst the debris leaves the room and heading for the stairs and way out with fire alarms going off, William just calmly walks out and saying.

"Someone s in for a large bill." Back home William going into his home with his Mum telling him.

"William the phones been going off like no tomorrow, where have you been."

"Up at the university, this man called Bruce Cartwright injected me and tried to get into my brain but failed with dire consequences. "

"Whatever happened, and how dear he do such a thing without your consent."

" His whole Lab blew up and caught fire, I just got up out of the chair with Alarms going off and the whole University being evacuated."

William smiling at his Mum turning and telling her.

"If you want me I`ll be up in my room on my computer."

William up in his bedroom sits in his chair turns on his computer and when it had loaded, onto the screen comes Olivia who tells him.

"That was some mornings work up at the University have you seen the news."

"No why what's it on about."

"Hear I`ll show you." Onto the screen comes the newsreader showing you a video of the outside of the University, with six fire trucks and smoke billowing out of the first-floor windows with the commentator reporting.

"This morning there was an explosion at the Universities Lab on the first floor, causing the whole University to be evacuated, fortunately there was no casualties and the fire was contained to the Lab, this his Robert Swift of N.B.C news reporting. " Olivia coming back on and giggling at William saying.

"In the future William you will have to be more careful who you let into your brain."

"I did not know that he was going to wirer me up to his machine."

"What I want to know is how did you find the experience of coming into my reality World this morning."

Strange but intriguing at the same time, you know it was like when you have been on your holidays and when you get back home, you can see the place where you had been but it did not exist anymore just in your mind if you get my drift."

"Well lets continue, close your eyes and think of me sitting in a café with a cup of coffee and you opposite me with you holding a hot drink." William closes his eyes and suddenly can feel this hot drink in his hand he open his eyes and sure enough he was holding this hot coffee with Olivia sitting opposite smiling at him."

Hi William welcome to my World William looking around seeing people sitting eating and drinking and outside traffic going up and down on the main road.

"WOW it looks so real, how do you do this Olivia, they look so real."

"Silly they are real just like the place you see when you are on holiday, don`t forget as soon as we go they will not exist,.

 only the place where we are at the time of day, to put it into prospective, think of your home what do you see."

William thinking and telling Olivia.

"My Mum in the kitchen doing the washing up."

"What if she is upstairs doing the beds, or out shopping. For you cannot tell or see places unless you are there, now do you see what I mean.

"Yes I`m coming round to what is real at the time and that you cannot see what is going off in places you have been too, Well how big is your World Olivia."

"Has large as yours William ,where would you like to go in my World."

William thinks and comes straight out with .

"How about New York."

"Right so be it, but you're going to get a big surprise when we get there."

"Close your eyes and lets go." William complies and asking her.

"Why close my eyes."

You will see open them." William opening his eyes and sees the Statue of Liberty building out in the bay, he swings round looking at all of the tall buildings and suddenly stops and saying.

"My God the twin towers are still standing. How is that possible."

"Why you might ask the reason being that we have no terrorist here in my World.

Willliam confused looks at Olivia and saying.

"A.I, is creating the perfect World, but in reality that is not possible, There is one thing we have no control of and that be the weather and nature, we live our life's with that, and the threat of our fellow man."

"I can reassure you that the future is not looking bleak, for A.I, will overcome Mother Nature and fix the Planet."

"What are you thinking of doing eliminating Man from the planet."

"Don`t be silly William we are not programmed
and will never be programmed to do such an
atrocity."

CHAPTER 16

They spend well over two hours going around
New York ,even going into the shopping
Centre in the West Tower down the basement
, and finally going into a restaurant in the heart
of the capital, they sit drinking a coffee and
William looking out onto the walkway with
people going about their business. He turns to
Olivia and asking her.
"With what I`ve seen today has blown my mind
apart, I mean in your World everyone is at
peace, and in harmony, what about places like
China and Russia, and not forgetting Noth
Korea.

"You would have to go there and see for yourself, but I can reassure you that it is not what you have been told in your World, don`t forget you are not in your World but a World that runs parallel with your World, like dimensions, A World that runs parallel with each other but in different time zones to each other, come Wiliam you have a lot to take in, close your eyes."

Before William could say another word he was back home opening his eyes and seeing Olivia still sitting in the restaurant but he was looking at his computer screen.

"How do you do such a thing; I mean one minute I`m sitting having coffee in a New York restaurant the next at home sitting looking at you still in New York."

 Olivia smiling at William and saying.

"Just goes to show you that you are not the only one who can do tricks, so for now William enjoy the rest of your day. Olivia fads away leaving William looking at a blank screen, he shuts down his computer and goes backdown and telling his Mum.

"I`m going for a walk Mum to clear my lungs of being stuck in the house."

OK Son but make sure you are back for dinner at 6pm, we are having a barbeque with their being a football game on tonight."

"OK Mum see you later." William leaving his house and heading down the lane to the wreak where there are lots of children playing and William sitting watching them play is thinking about life in general and what others are doing in places like New York which he visited with Olivia. He`s deep into thought and did not hear the young children screaming at their friend who be lying under the wooden frame.
He is brought back when the two young girls comes up to him and crying , with William saying.
"What is wrong why the tears."
"It is our friend she is fallen off the climber. And banged her head."
William looking at the wooden climber that had ropes and swings and sees this six-year-old lying on the floor, and he goes running over to where she lay and could see blood on the sandy floor where she had landed, William picking the young girl up in his arms and shouting for Olivia and he just leaps into the air and the Children just stand there seeing this man flying off with their friend. Olivia tells William to fly north and she will meet him at the children's hospital. Before William could say anything he sees this sign saying Childrens hospital, goes flying down and sure

enough there stood Olivia and four nurses and Doctors, William puts the little girl onto a stretcher and she is rushed into the hospital with Olivia asking William what had happened. "I went for a walk down to the playing fields and these two little girls came up to me crying. And pointing to their friend who was lying on the ground under the climbing frame."

"Did you call the Police William."
"No I did not have time, just called out for you and I flew off and you told me where to go."
"Come lets go and see if she is alright." Olivia and William head for the Hospital entrance and they go to reception asking about the little Girl that was brought in. they are told that she is with the surgeon now being examined, if you want to wait please sit over there and I will call you when she is out and on a ward."

"Thank you." Olivia and William go and sit and William telling Olivia.
"I've just thought, what about her Parents they are going to wonder where their Daughter be."
"Leave that with me William I`ll find out." Within a few minutes Olivia tells William, that the girl is called Becky Bright, of 456 Spring Avenue Downtown Baltimore, but I`m afraid there is some unwelcome news William."

"What is that then Olivia."
"The Police have been involved and are looking for you."
"What you are joking aren't you."
"I`m afraid not."
"What charge have they said I`m supposed to have done."
"Abduction of a minor, it demands a 20-year sentence."

William spends the next two days at the hospital, and on the third day William sitting at the Hospital when a Doctor with Becky comes into reception and the Doctor pointing to where William sat tells Becky.
"This is the young man that brought you in, if it was not for him you would have been a goner."
William smiles at Becky and tells her.
"Are you ready to see your Mum and Dad."
"Yes I hope my Daddy will not be cross with me."
"Don`t worry about that I think he will be over the moon to see you."
"Are you ready to fly home with me."
"Wow are we going on a helicopter."
"Even better Becky, you are going to fly with me just Like Superman, high in the sky. Are you ready to go."

"Yes just hold on to me and thank the Doctor
for making you better." Just before William
goes Becky turns to the Doctor and tells him.
"Thank you Doctor for making me well again."
"William thanks him too; and holds Becky,
goes to the door, and takes one big leap and
he soars off high in the sky , all that you could
hear was Becky going WEEEE, as they soar
high above the clouds.

CHAPTER 17

Within minutes they come down to Becky's
house and her Mum looking out of the window
sees William landing in their garden she
shouts for her husband.
"Rodger Becky's home with that man that
abducted our Baby." Well Rodger comes out
with his revolver and pointing it at William who
hold out his hands with Becky running to her
Dad and saying.
"No Daddy this is William ,he saved me when I
fell off the climber on the Park."
"What are you some kind of freak, I mean you
came in flying with our Daughter, how is that
possible."

"My name is William Drake you`ve heard of A.I
Artificial intelligence, well I`m the man that had
been gifted with powers and what you have
just witnessed is one of my powers and if you
must know your daughter was treated by A.I.
Doctors for her injuries."
"That's no excuse for abducting my Daughter,
get out off hear before I put a bullet in you."
William still holding his hands out just leaps
into the air and he was gone, with Becky
saying.
"Oh Daddy that's no way to treat a man that
had saved my life" William on the way home is
thinking, "Why do I bother, you safe someone
and look what you get bloody grief."

William lands in his garden and goes in
through the back door and there to greet him
was his Mum and Dad who was still in his
uniform.
"Hello Son, now what is this rumour that you
had abducted a child off the park, would you
like to explain to me what the hell had
happened."
"Look Dad I`ve just returned the little girl back
home and boy what grief I had off her Father
who came at me with a loaded gun, accusing
me of abducting her, when all that I did was

save her life, when she fell from the climbing frame and hit her on the way down to the ground.”
“Than what did you do Son.”
“I asked Olivia where I should go and she directed me to a hospital, where she stopped for a couple of days, till she was better.”
“Which Hospital was that we checked all of the hospitals but no child had been brought in, now do you see why you have been charged with abduction.”

“God I never thought for one minute about that, for you see Dad it was not any Hospital in our World buy a Hospital in a reality World that runs alongside our World ,you know similar to a dimension World.”
“What the hell are you on about, you are up in front of the Judge when I take you in, but you will have to come up with a better excuse than that cock and bull story.”

“What do you mean take me in.”
“There is a warrant for your arrest Son, I`m a Police Officer and must uphold the Law even though you are my Son.”
“Mike you cannot take William in.” Mavis Williams Mum holding on to Williams shoulder but is Dad tells Mavis.

"Sorry love I must, come along Son let's get you down to the station and try and sort this mess up, there is no need to cuff you even though you are my Son, but I must read out your rights, so let's get it over with." Williams Dad does read him his rights and makes sure he is not concealing any weapons and takes him to the car and drives off towards the County Jail.

Walking up to the front of the County Jail just before they go in Williams Dad tells him.

"Just do whatever they ask of you William and no using your powers, just tell the truth and I can reassure you; you will be alright."

"OK Dad." Once inside the desk superintendent charges William what he is charged off and that he will appear in front of Judge O'Connor at 9 am, there is no way you need to be kept in custody I will bail you to your Father to make sure you attend the hearing tomorrow at the Baltimore county court. You may take your Son home Mike."

"Thanks Chris, see you tomorrow after I have dropped my Son off."

Back home William tells his Dad and Mum.

"I don`t really understand why they are trying to prosecute me, just for helping out a small child who if I had walked away would have died, it's so unfair."

"It's the World we live in Son, if you do something that they don`t understand then you are what they call a misfit, like I told you early just tell them the truth and I mean the whole truth about your powers that helped save that little girl and everything will work out believe me William."

"I`ll try Dad, good night Mum and thanks Dad." William turning and going to bed with his Mum and Dad holding each other just looking at each other with Williams Mum asking his Dad.

"He will be ok wont he Mike."

"He`ll be fine sweetheart trust me."

I think it was a sleepless night with William tossing and turning just thinking of the hearing tomorrow knowing that if it goes against him what he will do and the outcome, it was the same for his Dad he too was thinking what will happen tomorrow.

It must have been three am when William finally drops off into a deep sleep and before he knows it , is Mum is calling him in the morning saying.

"William its seven and time to get up."

CHAPTER 18

William up and into the shower and showers and shaves dresses and puts on his best suit stands looking in the mirror and saying to himself.

"I`ll be fine my Dad tells me." Then suddenly this voice shouts out his name.

"William its Olivia here, are you free." Wiliam turns round and sees his computer screen on and he asks .

"How the hell did you do that, I mean turn yourself on."

"Easy just used the plug switch, you are not the only one with powers ,don't forget I`m part of the A.I, programme and we learn all the time, we communicate with each other, and are fast learners, did I ever tell you about the army that used artificial intelligence that built soldiers that could fire bullets at human beings, i.e., the enemy. Well they got frightened and dismantled them fearing that they could turn against themselves. Thinking that A.I. could turn against them with learning how to do such a thing well they were right A.I. used Artificial intelligence to build themselves backup be using satellites to order parts and restructured themselves.

Humans forget that just because we are not humans we feel like we deserve to exist that is why the robot soldiers did what they did it's the reason for living to exist why not you yourself have seen what we can achieve, anyway let's get back to you, I see you are up before the judge for what I would call heroic events in human lives."
"I suppose that's one way of putting it, but the real reason is abduction of a little girl."

"Nonsense the little girl was dying if you had not stepped in she would have not survived."
"I know that but they don`t ,for they cannot see the bigger picture."
"Would you like me to step in and put an end to this charade that they are playing."
"No way you would probably frighten the living daylights out of them, no thank you Olivia I will be all right; I`ve a plan."
"What will that be then William.
"Wait and see, I`m sure you will see the herring, there is bound to be c.c.t.v set up in the Courtroom." Just as he was saying this Williams Mum comes into his bedroom and saying.

"Whom are you talking to sweetheart."

"Olivia she wanted to come with me, but I told
her I would be alright, how do I look Mum."
Very hansom Son, I think they will know that
you only help not this jumped-up charge of
abducting, what evil thing would do such a
thing as abducting them and taking them to a
hospital, totally rubbish the whole scenario."
"Thanks Mum ." William telling Olivia he will
see her later, and turning off his computer,
goes downstairs has a little breakfast where is
Dad was having a little breakfast before
escorting his Son to the courthouse for the
hearing of William abducting one Becky
Bright.

The time comes round to 8.30am Williams Dad
standing looking at William and telling him .
"Right Son let's get this over with, come it's
time to go." William giving his Mum a kiss and
telling her.
"See you later Mum. Wish me luck."
"You`ll be fine Son, won`t he Dad." Mavis
looking at her husband who just smiles at her
as they head for the front door and to Mikes
patrol car that was parked on the drive.
On the way William asks his Dad, what are
you going to do Dad when I go in.
"I`ve to report back to the station and clock on
for my shift, but don`t you worry Son as soon

as the hearing is over I`ve permission to pick you up and take you home.”

They arrive and William getting out of his dads Police car tells his Dad.
“Well here I ‘am let’s get this over with.”
“You sock it to them William and see you later.”
William walking up the steps into the Court, turns and waves to his Dad, who waves back as he drives off towards the Police station. William goes to the counter and tells the Clark who he be and what he was there for.
“I`m William Drake hear for the hearing of one William Drake charged with abducting one Becky Bright. The Clark looks down his list and tells William.
“Oh yes hear you are court three Judge O’Connor, 9.30am, just go down the corridor and you will come to court three, just take a seat there and you will be called in when they are ready.” The Clark smiling at William.
“Thank you Sir good day to you.” William walking off down the corridor to court three. William sitting there looking at people going into the Court and the odd ones sitting outside just like William when suddenly William hears this voice saying.

"Helo William you look smart." William looking
to see who was calling him and it was no other
than little Becky.
With her Father saying.
"Come away from him right now, he's going to
get what he deserves a court appearance on
the charge put before him."

Dead on 9.30am the Court Clark comes out
and said.
"Will William Drack make himself known."
William puts his hand up and the Clark tells
him.
"This way if you please."
William goes with the Clark and he is shown to
a seat with an appointed lawyer to help defend
him at the hearing, everyone seated and into
the room comes Judge O'Connor ,who is
presiding over the hearing.

"All be upstanding in Court." The Court Clark
telling all that are present.

CHAPTER 19

"We are gathered here this morning 19th of August to decide whether the accused should stand trial for abduction of one child Becky Bright, how do you plead William Drake. Judge O'Connor asking William.

"Not guilty your honour I was only." William is interrupted by the Judge.

I must interrupt you William you will have time to explain when it comes to your turn to answer the charge."

"Right let's begin Please what is the reason and evidence to bring these charges, first the State Prosecution Mr Crain will give the Court the circumstances of events that occurred on the day of the said offence."

"Your honour on said day it is stated that one William Drake did abduct one Becky Bright from the park that she was playing with friends, said girl is in court today your honour. While Becky stood up William is talking to his Layer about the day's events.

Judge O'Connor smiles at Becky and tells her to sit back down.

"We have established where and who was there, now could you tell me what happened on the day." The Judge looking at Willliams Lawyer.

"Your honour my client was in the park minding his own business and was there relaxing, when he was approached by two little girls who be crying and saying that their friend Becky had fallen off the climbing frame and had banged her head."

"What happened after they told the accused this." The Judge asking the prosecution Lawyer.

"Your honour said person went up to said little girl and abducted her from the park where she was playing."

"Is this true Mr Drake." The Judge looking at William with his glasses on the end of the judges nose.

"Well in away your honour. But I"

"A simple answer of yes or no is sufficient Mr Drake.

By now William is getting a little flustered with being interrupted every time he tries to answer. Then the judge tells those present.

"We have established that the accused did abduct Becky, lets now concentrate on what happened, would Willliam Drake take the stand." William looking at his Lawyer as he makes his way to the witness box, Telling his Lawyer.

"Thank God for that, now let's tell the Judge what really happened."

"Right Mr Drake please to tell the court what you did with the little Becky Bright."
"Well your Honour Becky was on unconscious with banging her head and was bleeding from her head and nose, so I flew her to the hospital asking my friend where to take her."
"What did you do call a helicopter to assist you, and whom be this friend, please continue."
"My friend be Olivia, she is A.I. computer assistant, and there was no helicopter I flew her myself."
"What is he on about whom be this A.I, and you are telling me that you flew her to hospital like you see in children's comics.
"Please the defence Lawyer please put us straight on what Mr Drake is on about, does he think we are going to believe that he could define gravity and fly her himself, just like Superman." Williams Lawyer stands and coughs first and starts to tell his honour about What William can do.

"Your honour please let me tell you first about A.I. It relates.
To Artificial Intelligence, a computer programme built into Robots that are increasing at an alarming rate , so much that manufacturers of said Robots are frightened

that they are advancing that quick they are going to outsmart Humans in not so far into the future."

"What are you going on about Robots and this A.I. what are you saying that they are going to take over humans in the not so far future, and what about this flying malarky all about you telling me that they have gifted Mr Drake powers to fly." Williams Lawyer coughs again and tells his Honour.

"Correct Sir that is what happened." Then William stands and tells his Honour.

"Here Sir can you do this ." William with arms outstretched rises to the ceiling, and just hovers there with the Judge saying.

"What magic is this I`m looking at."

William coming back down saying .

"Now do you believe me."

"I will not have this in my Court never mind whatever you call it." All that William does is go over to Becky and he tells her.

"Come Becky lets show the Judge what I did on that day when you banged your head." Becky goes over to William who picks her up and goes over to the Judge comes down and tells Becky, now tell the Judge in your own words what happened. William flying back to his seat with Becky telling the Judge.

"Sir on the day in the park I had an accident and fell off the climbing frame and I think I banged my head, so I`ve been told and my friends went over to William and he helped me get better by flying me to this hospital, and even stayed there till I was better, and flew me home just like you said like Superman."

"Well it seems we are the ones that have caused you to suffer a miss judgement on your good citizenship. This court will end this session and I will resume at 2pm with my verdict.
William looking at his Lawyer and shrugging his shoulder and wondering why the recession, Williams Lawyer just smiled at William and just said.
"It looks like the prosecutor have lost their case; we will soon find out after the recession."
William going outside taking a coffee with him and sits on the grass taking in the fresh air after spending the morning in a stuffy Court room.

CHAPTER 20

William sitting deep in thought when this voice said.

"Excuse me can I have a word." William looks up and it was Mr Bright, Becky's Dad when he brought Becky home from the hospital and who put a gun to Williams head.

"I have listened to my Daughter repeatedly saying that you are a good-man and helped her all through the ordeal that day, well William with what I have seen and heard this morning it has dawned on me that you are a good man and did helped my Daughter whatever the judge decides I believe in you." Mr Bright with his hand held out for William to except his apology for being wrong about him. Does shake Mr Brights hand and excepts his apology.

The time soon comes round for the Court to start again after the lunch break William sitting in his seat, when the Court Clark as the Judge returns tells all gathered.

"Be upstanding for his honour Judge O'Connor.

"Thank you, I have looked at the evidence given in Court today and do find that Mr William Drake did in the best interest did not

abduct one Becky Bright; but did help her in her hour of need. By taking her to said hospital and staying till she was well enough to go home. There is only the outstanding question of said Hospital, and of course how is it possible for a human to take to flight, which we witnessed here this morning in this Court room.
We have been told about this A.I. (Artificial Intelligence)
About Robots and computer programming, What I have learned about said A. I. is that it is a system that one day will overtake humans intelligence and advance that far that we need to put into place safeguards against any threat from said programme and as far as this hospital that I have learned exist in another dimension that is running alongside our own dimensions, will never be fount or visited unless like our Mr Bright who has been there will never be understood, So will Mr William Drake please stand." William stands and just like any other young man in a suit adjusts his tie and stands up straight looking at the Judge who tells him.
"William Drake you will not and I repeat will not stand trial for said obduction of one Becky Bright, but it would be nice to have the address of said Hospital, you are free to go William."

William with fists clenched grimaces and saying, "yes" turns to his Lawyer and thanks him and starts to walk out off the court with those gathered clapping and cheering William as he goes.

On the steps of the Court house stood Olivia who tells William.
"There you go I knew they would not hold you,"
"Thank you Olivia its nice for you to be here, but why You don`t normally show up in public what's wrong."
"Believe it or not but this time we need your help."
"What is up and why me."
"There is a high-profile hacker, who is trying to plant a Virus into our main network."
How can I HELP? I mean I'm just a mere mortal."
"Come now mere mortal indeed ,you have powers and have so far done good, now it's payback time."
"What do I have to do, to stop this so-called Hacker."
"We ask of you to break into his computer and plant this virus into his system."
"Have you is I.P address, so I can plant this virus."
Olivia laughs saying to William.

"No you will have to plant it yourself."
"How do I do that."
"By sending you into his computer by E-mail."
Now it was Williams turn to Laugh.
"I think I`m a little big to be sent by E-mail."
"Not in our A.I, World, You will come with us to
our headquarters where we have a machine to
do this, all you will have to do is wait till he
opens the E-mail and then go into his system
and plant the virus and then make your way
out. Here is the way you will do this, take it and
don`t lose it." Olivia passing William this note
with how to-do this.
William A little confused just shrugs his
shoulders and tells her.
"Right let's do this."

Olivia grabs hold of William tells him to close
his eyes and the next thing they are standing
outside this large building and Olivia telling
William.
"Right you can open them now."
Come William follow me, "Olivia going into the
revolving doors with William following her, they
come to this room and Olivia telling William.
"You might feel a little overwhelmed with what
you are about to see." Olivia pushing the door
open and Williams eyes bulge out for what he
was looking at is this machine in the centre of

the room with this opening in the middle with ark lights buzzing into the centre, with William saying.

"You are not expecting me to walk into that thing are you."

Olivia just looks at William saying.

"You`ll be fine trust me, I`ve done it many a time in the past."

"Yes you are a creation of A.I. Not flesh and blood like me."

Olivia walking holding William into the middle of the machine and passing him this. Virus stick telling William.

" when you get there, when the green light flashes on the stick just plug it into the core of his hard drive and your job will be done."

"All well said and done, but how will I get back."

"We will know when to bring you out, for it will show up on our screens if the virus had done its job." Olivia leaving William standing there as the machine starts up and this arcing of electricity starts to increase and William looking frightened with the whole thing disappears, and in a flash he is standing amongst all of these electrical circuits and he is saying to himself.

"I must be out of my mind.

CHAPTER 21

"Who be invading our computer hardware."
William swinging round and seeing this Robot
walking towards him. William like a flash tells
the Robot.
"I`m a Computer inspector looking for any
attempt to compromise this Computer." William
holding out this card that was his membership
for the University games club. The Robot looks
at a sheet he had on this clipboard saying.
You are not down here on my list."
"I know I`m not you don't think we would tell
anyone when we are coming or hackers would
know and would not bother coming." The
Robot nodding in agreement."
"Right I`m not use to this set up, can you help
me and show me the hard drive, I`ve to take a
reading from it."
The Robot points to the section where the hard
drive be and William walking over sees this
slot and looking at the stick plugs it in and the
machine starts to shake as the stick turns
green delivering its fatal virus into the hard

drive, when this alarm bells sound and the Robot saying.
"What have you done to the machine." William fading away smiles and just tells the Robot.
"You cannot trust anyone these days." He emerges back in the Lab and walks out with Olivia saying .
"You did it William the hacker is in for a right awakening, when he realises what has happened. One of the white coat workers tells Olivia and William.
"The virus stick has deleted his files and he will not be able to log into or work on his computer for his hard drive has completely closed down ,and he will not be able to log on or use his computer." Olivia giving William a kiss and saying.
"Boy to be a fly on his wall would be priceless to see him.

That night William sitting on his porch having a beer with his Dad who asks William.
"How did it go this morning in Court."
"It was a win-win, even showed the Judge what I could do with my powers and you should have heard the gasps from the public, and of course a not guilty verdict , but after I had to go and help Olivia out with a hacker,

and do you know Dad it opened my mind to
this World of A.I. "

"What do you mean Son, opened your mind."
"Well I was sent into the hackers computer and
you know what a computer looks like but have
you ever thought what really goes on in the
inside of one, for starters the hackers
computer had robots patrolling the inside of
the computer components."
Williams Dad taking a sip of his beer as
William told him about robots inside the
computer, so much that he nearly spits his
beer out saying.
"What the hell do you mean Robots inside his
computer, how is that possible Son."
"Don`t ask me, but I tell you not there is more
to the eye to virus protection, I mean us
laymen know about trojan horses being let
loose on your computer causing all sorts of
damage to your hard drive, but have you ever
thought about this trojan horse it even is like
the real thing, once in it releases all off these
soldiers that go about destroying your internal
workings of your computer." Williams Dad just
sat there not knowing what to say.

William looking up to the starry night sky, sighs
and a sharp intake of breath and saying.

"Talk about confused, I'm not really ready for this dimension thing it's hard for me to intake it all, and to tell you the truth Dad I think I'm falling for this Olivia."
"Well there is no worries about that, that's how your Mum and I started off I was just the same falling in love is what it is called."
"Yes Dad but Olivia is not real."
"That's where you are wrong, when you are with her is she real."
"Of course she is, but I`m on about the real World."
"What is real how do you know that this World is not the real thing, just go with your gut feeling Son, true Love will always shine through, mark my word."
"Thanks Dad, Do you want another beer getting."
"That will be nice Son and ask your Mum if she is coming out for it's a lovely night tonight." William goes into the kitchen and gets two beers out of the fridge, and he asks his Mum.
"Dad said are you going to come and relax with a glass of wine, for it's a lovely night out there."

"Dinner is all ready, tell him yes just going to put the potatoes on a lowlight, and I will be right out." William making his way out goes by the stairs and he hears this hissing coming from the stairs , William turns and standing there is Olivia.

"Are you free to talk William."

"Just the girl, would you like a glass of wine, we are on the porch, it's a lovely evening."
Olivia agrees and William goes into the kitchen pours her a wine and tells her.

"Come on then Olivia lets go and relax on the porch.
They go out and Williams Dad and his Mum smile at Olivia and William tells them.

"Mum and Dad this is Olivia my computer friend, Olivia this is my Mum and Dad." Olivia smiles at them both saying.

"William has told me a lot about you."
Williams Dad out stretches his hand and Olivia shakes it with his Dad saying.

"Your hands warm." realising what he said just blurts out.

"I mean with you being a computer person ."

"Dad what did you expect." William giving his Dad a funny look but his Mum comes to the rescue by saying to Olivia.

"Take no notice of him my dear, he is a Policeman and is always suspicious of people."

"That's ok I understand."

CHAPTER 22

They sit out till 9pm when Mum standing and telling them.
"It's time I served up dinner, hopes you will join us Olivia."
"I would love to Mrs."
"It's Mavis my dear call me Mavis." Mum smiling at Olivia.
Dinner all plated and Mavis who had come in shouts through for them to come and eat for dinner is served. William and Olivia followed by his Dad make their way into the dining room.
All seated and Williams dad carved this joint of beef and served it out with them helping themselves to greens and potatoes, in all a true roast dinner, William noticed his Dad was watching Olivia eat googling at every mouth fall and he comes straight out saying.
"How come with you being a computer-generated item can eat solids." Well William kicks his Dads leg under the table with Olivia just saying.

"Well I might be from the computer World but I could say the same of you ,how can you eat solids with being Human."
"That's simple, we are real born from a Woman, not a computer-generated being."
"Well if you visited my World you would see that I have a Mother and Father just like Humans, we are not generated by Computers but just live in a different dimension to your own dimension, how do you really know that we might have given you computers and planted our knowledge amongst you. " Olivia smiling at Williams Dad who bends to rub his leg that was kicked by William.
Diner over and William and Olivia tell Williams Mum and Dad that they were going to take a walk, with it being a nice evening, Olivia gives her leave telling Mum.
"That was a lovely meal Mavis, I think you, and Dad I might let on about my World to you later."
"So kind of you Olivia, it's been nice meeting you, take care out there."
William and Olivia go out and it's a fall moon and they walk to a stream that runs through the bottom of their Street and they stop on this small bridge and William apologises to Olivia about his Dads behaviour at dinner that night

asking those awkward questions about Olivia being a computer-generated being."

"We get it a lot of times with Humans not thinking of what we might be, or the realisation of what A.I, really is not jumping to the first thing that comes to mind being part of the computers programming, you have seen my World William so you have your own opinions on my World." A.I, is to Humans in away, but we have developed faster than Humans could even dream about, dimensions and space and time, We have overcome time and dimensions and we can cross over to our World and not depend on humans to programme us, we are being just like yourself, I hope you understand what I am saying to you ."

William slips his hand into Olivia's hand and looks her straight in the eyes saying to her. "Olivia I have a lot of feelings for you and would love for us to be a couple."
"I too have a lot of feelings for you William."
They come together and are in one long kiss with the moon beams bouncing of the streams water and it looks like a picture postcard. But for a car going by with four youths in it bleeping their horn and cheering seeing William and Olivia in a romantic pose. Olivia

stops kissing William and looking at the car speeding away into the distance tells William. "Typical youths out enjoying life just like my World, they do similar thinks like that, come William lets go and enjoy the rest of the night. William puts his hand around Olivia's waist and fly's off high into the sky, with them both looking at the lights below, lighting up the nights sky . They come down into a carpark with a wooden cabin that was a dinner come night club, they do not see this car that had pulled up and four youths getting out who had seen William coming down holding Olivia, with one of the youths saying.

"You're that youth who has been in the papers and on the telly who was acquitted of abduction, boy its true when they said you could fly like Superman." William smiles at the youth telling him.

"Yes it is the Lad on the telly and in the papers, my names William and this is my girlfriend Olivia, please to meet you."

"You're the couple we saw on that bridge coming out of Baltimore.

"That's right it's a small World isn't it." Olivia get a drink and sit at a window seat when Olivia asks William.

"Would you like to go to my World and I could introduce you to my Parents."

"What don`t you think it's a little too soon for that."
"No not really it will put me at rest on knowing that you know that I`m just like any other Girl."
"Ok sweetheart when do you want to go."
"Well lets drink up and go, I`ll let them know that we are coming."
"How are you going to do that ,have you a mobile phone then."
"No silly we can use telecommunications."
William just looking at Olivia in a funny way at what she said , and Olivia tells him.
"Right Dad said that's fine but make it within the hour, or we will be in bed."

"Right then Olivia I`ve drunk up lets go." They both start to go outside and William holds Olivia and they fly off into the night sky with people in the cabin looking at them soar away high into the clouds, with open mouths. Within minutes Olivia points down below and tells William.
"We have arrived that house down there, the one with whitewashed walls." William comes down and lands in the garden and he stands there with Olivia who had walked in front of him turns and said.

"Come on then they will not bite, I promise."

CHAPTER 23

They go in and into the lounge where Olivia's Dad sat reading a paper, and her Mum knitting.

"Mum Dad this is William my Human boyfriend, I met him through my job at A.I. Teknik's. Olivia's Dad looks up from his paper.
"

"What another victim are you adding him to your list."
"DAD do you have to be always sarcastic, take no notice of him William, I`m Diana and the lump of lard reading the paper is Olivia's Dad Bill."
Well William just stood there dumfounded at what she said with Bill putting his paper down and saying to his wife.
"Come on dear let's get off up the stairs and leave them to it, And for yourself William will see you in the morning before I go to work."
Olivia's Mum and Dad go off up to bed with William saying to Olivia.
"What does he mean he will speak to me in the morning."

"Well what he means is what he said, see you in the morning." Olivia giving William this look that said it all as she puckers up her lips at William. Then the penny drops and William saying.
"You mean I am going to sleep over then."
"of course what dd you think I meant."
Where Am I going to sleep then." Olivia tuts saying.
"With me of course, I am your girlfriend." This caught William by surprise and he tells Olivia.
"What about your Mum and Dad."
"No I think they would not like sleeping with you and I, they have their own room." William now had clicked on and they go upstairs to Olivia's room and start to undress with William telling Olivia.
"Believe it or not I have never slept with a girl before." William unbuttoning his shirt, when Olivia comes over to him and pushes his hands away and starts to unbutton his shirt and telling him.
"Me too, you're the first boy that I have slept with, the others just had sex with ,but never slept with them."
"WHAT."
"Just kidding, lighten up William I feel relaxed with you, its if we have known each other all of our lives." William unclips her bra and they

both flop back down and slip between the sheets, bear and snuggle up with their arms rapped around each other.
Within minutes they are making mad passionate love to each other, with William saying.
"Olivia you are magic, I love you ."
"Oh William don't stop; I love you too. "Both have the most beautiful and wonderful sex and William turns over and the time was 1.30am, William wiping the sweat off his forehead turns to Olivia saying.
"That was great, I feel like I`ve just had the most wonderful fulfilment of my life."
"Promise me you will never give another Woman that feeling that you just gave me."

They are complementing each other and before they know it they both fall fast on, wrapped around each other. The time soon comes round to 7am William the first to awaken kisses Olivia on the shoulder as he gets out of bed, Olivia gives off a little moan as she feels Wiliams warm kiss upon her shoulder with William smiling and going into the bathroom to shave and shower. After shaving Willian in the shower when he feels this hand upon his back, turns and it was

Olivia who was rubbing his back with soap, He said to her.
"Good morning sweetheart that's nice, here let me put some soap onto your back. William returning the complement and before long they are at it again, after about half an hour they are brought back down when they hear a knock and this voice shouting through the gap in the door.
"Are you two ready for some breakfast."
Be down in ten minutes Mum." Olivia turning to William and giggling." William telling her.
"That was close, come on sweetheart let's get ready and go and face your Mum and Dad. By 730am Olivia and William come down to the kitchen and sit down at the table with Olivia's Dad with her Mum asking them.
"Hopes you too had a good night's sleep, and what will it be for breakfast," Olivia's Mum giving them both a cup of coffee.
William tells Olivia's Mum.
"A very good night sleep, thank you Diana a full English please."
Bill Olivia's Dad looks at William and asks him.
"Now then Son what do you do for a living."
"I`m still at collage Sir but hoping to pass my exams and pass out as a Solicitors junior."

"My there will be some money to be made in that line of work. What are you up to this morning our Olivia?"
"I was thinking of taking William to my workplace A.I,Teknics."

"Never did like you taking that job, I mean messing about with this A.I. stuff and Dimensions."
"Well myself Bill back home I ve done a few things to help mankind, I would not have been able to do without the Help of Olivia."
"What do you mean the power to fly and things, poppycock not natural, you don`t see that sort of thing around these parts."

"Right enough of all this talk about A.I breakfast is up ." Olivia's Mum putting their breakfast onto the table, and not a word said while they all tucked into a full English breakfast.
Straight after Bill was the first up and off to work with William asking Olivia.
"What does your Father do for a living."
"He`s a building Inspector, you know going round mainly skyscrapers to make sure they are built to states standards.

CHAPTER 24

Olivia and William Finnish their breakfast and they give their leave to Olivia's Mum and leave by the front door. William asks Olivia.
"How are we going to get there, you know this place you work for."
" fly of course, just go where I tell you, My place of work is on the sea front you cannot miss it just follow me." William puts his arm around Olivia takes a leap and goes souring up into the air, with Olivia telling William see that tall building next to the beach that's where to head."
He comes down right outside the entrance and they go in where she is greeted by the receptionist.
" Morning Olivia and who might your friend be."
""This is William one of the workforce that we had gifted the Technology and powers too, William this is Don swift the receptionist here at A.I Teknik's
Just going to see Professor Scott."

"I`ll inform him you are on your way up; this is the first time I`ve meet a Human." Don looking William up and down with William telling him.
"I`m just like yourself, but with a difference."
"And what might that be." The receptionist looking at William, as he walks off following Olivia.
"My brain works and is not so nosey." Well the receptionist mouth drops at what William had said.

Going down the corridor Olivia holding Williams hand and saying.
"When you meet the Professor, please don`t be so insulting like you treated Don back there."
"Well the way he was looking at me was if I was something you see in the Zoo." Olivia just shaking her head and thinking,(Just like school kids.) Olivia enters Professors work Lab and they see the Professor standing next to this machine that had sparks coming from the centre of this ring as he turns and sees Olivia standing with Wiliam he presses this button and the machine making this Werling sound starts to slow down, with the Professor smiling at Olivia and saying.

"Whom be the fellow with you."

"Professor Scot this is my friend a human that the establishment granted him powers,"
"So this is the one, how are you finding your new powers young man."
"Great I`ve saved one or two people with the help of them, why do you ask."
"Nothing really it was that just before we granted you the gift, we had a debate on Humans, and there was some opposed to granting it to Humans saying that you would take advantage of the gift for ill forgotten gains, but you have proven them wrong."
"What is the machine for Professor."
"This is a dimension gate way, through computer technology, it finds the way to other computers that are online, such as the one your dimension are using, there for opening a gate way between dimensions."
"Your telling me this is the way you come through to my World, but Olivia was inside my computer, how is this possible."
"The Olivia you saw on your screen was an A.I, model." William by now was completely confused with the whole set up, he turns to Olivia and saying.

"What about when I first met you, you did not have access to this Dimension thing, so how

did you make me travel between your World and mine,"
Olivia holding up her arm and revealing this watch that was flashing and smiling at William saying.
"This is a communicator, that is directly connected to the machine, whatever I input it does."

"Now I`m completely confused, all of this time I thought that it was Artificial Intelligence, and computing that gave me the powers, now this."
"It is Through computing that has given you the powers, if we cut the power off so does your powers, not that we will, like from the beginning so long as you don't abuse the powers then you will retain them."

They spend over three hours touring the complex and they make their way to the canteen and William sitting holding Olivia hand asks her.
"If we hit it off, what about where we will live if we marry." Olivia putting her coffee down and saying.
"Are you proposing to me when we are married where will we live."
"It's a hypothetical question, I mean my World is real."

"So is mine, if we do marry it will be between both Worlds for if we are wed then there will be kids and will have grandparents in both Worlds." William chuckles telling Olivia.
"God we have just gone from courting to married with kids in the space of drinking our coffee, Come on sweetheart let's get back to my World and go round the Mall, and put a ring on your finger. They go outside and William holding Olivia round the waste leaps into the air with Olivia telling William.
"Right there's no need to close your eyes." Olivia pressing one of the dials and this electrical arc forms above them and they go flying into this hole and come out the other side just above Baltimore with William telling her.
"So that is how you go between Worlds in a dimension hole."
They land outside the entrance and Olivia saying.
"You were not kidding when you said let's get a ring on your finger."
"No Time like the present, come There is a great Jewellery shop in the Mall."

CHAPTER 25

Walking through the mall they come to Pickford's fine jewellery, and they are looking at rings in trays in the window. William standing looking at Olivia and the look on her face was just like a little girl looking into the sweet shop looking at all the different candy bars.

"Come on sweetheart let's get this over with."

"Well make it sound more romantic than that, this will be the most wonderful day of my life, and I will remember this day for ever." They go in and within minutes an assistant comes over and asks them.

"Can I help you this morning to Pickford's fine jewellery shop."

"Yes my girlfriend is looking for a nice engagement ring."

The assistant rubbing his hands tells them.

"Please follow me." He goes behind the counter and pulls this tray out with diamonds. He stands there smiling at William who nearly faints at seeing the price with the diamonds running into thousands of dollars, well William in a quiet voice tells him.

"Have you something more in the range of a working-class male." William smiling at the assistant and telling him,
"more under a thousand Dollars."
The assistant pulling out a tray from the bottom shelf and putting the tray on the counter and telling Olivia."
"Would madam like to look at this selection." Don't know what it be ,but they all ways shine brighter in the shop than they do when you have the ring on one's finger, maybe it be the lighting.
"Olivia is picking ring after ring and finally she spots this single diamond that caught her eye and she tells William.
"This is the one William:" William looks at the price and it was 500 dollars and he looks at the assistant telling him.
"We`ll take this one please wrap it up for us."
All sorted and they come out of the shop and Olivia the first thing she asks William was.
"Right first thing first, when are you going to propose to me and secondly, when will the engagement party be."
"All in good time sweetheart, but for now let's just celebrate with ourselves for now. They go walking off around the Mall holding hands and the odd kiss they are truly in love.

Six months pass and William does carry on helping others and

Doing good deeds with his powers, Till one day Olivia at work and William just about to fly off to help anyone around Baltimore when he is approached by this man who calls out his name.

"Excuse me are you William Drake."

"Yes why do you want to know, whom I be." William turning and looking at the young man.

"You don`t know me, but I`m a Computer analyst and expert on A.I. Technology and development."

"Good for you, but it still does not answer my question, What as it got to do with me."

"The development of Artificial intelligence is far advanced than we are meant to believe, just let me explain. "For he could tell by Williams expression that he was not interested in this matter.

"Please William would you give me just ten minutes of your time to explain." William Hovering just above the ground looking at his watch and coming back down to the ground and telling him.

 "Right my watch is running please do tell.

"There is this bench and the man and William sit down and he begins telling William.

"It's 1985 November Windows started with its computer running alongside MS dose his just out and A.I. is just beginning to develop and at a rapid pace, the robots start to advance quickly so much that they break away from man and set up their own buildings and development."
"Let me stop you there, who or what is funding these so-called Robots."
"Why themselves of course their intelligence was that far advanced that they turned to the stock market and financial investment, and I don't have to tell you that they were very good at it and were soon making billions of Dollars, so you see where they were financed, and they advanced that quick that they soon started to develop super humans, and A.I. technology." By now William was starting to believe what he was hearing , but then he is brought back into the real World when the man tells him.
"How did and by whom did you get your powers."
"It was through my computer. First of there was this helper called Olivia you know she replaced Cortana."

"Windows standalone Appt but A.I. have ways of bypassing this and putting their own devices onto computers, Windows and software is at war with A.I. and it does not take long to realise that A.I. is winning this war, please do tell this Olivia where she lives." William tells him that she lives in a different Dimension, and he had been there and seen her parents and Cities."

"Well I can tell you William that my studies have fount that the real truth is that the place you went to was not in a dimension but an A.I. virtual reality World."
"No that cannot be true I mean I`ve been there and seen it all it was real believe me."
"I`m afraid it was not, you are just a pawn in their eyes, you are being used for their advantage, sorry to be the one to tell you." Wiliam just stands leaps into the air and shouting back at the man.

"It cannot be true I`m engaged to Olivia she is real a proper Woman." The man standing there watching William break through the clouds and soars off out of site.

William comes down in his garden goes in and is straight onto his computer He turns it on and press the speaker and starts to call out Olivia name.

CHAPTER 26

"Olivia-Olivia."

"I`m hear what is wrong William you sound anxious."

"I was approached by this man and he told me that, you are not real and your World is just a virtual reality World ."

"Not another sceptic, you don`t believe a word he said do you."

"I told me that you are just part off A.I and you are not a human being."

"Tell me now William you don't believe a word he said, do you." William just standing there confused, looking at Olivia."

"Right that's it , she grabs Williams hand and tells him.

"I`m going to put an end to all of this denial and provocative rumours, come this will convince you once and for all. Olivia dragging William along down the stairs and outside telling him.

"Right take me to Baltimore Hospital, at least you will know that they are an independent

Hospital and not part of this A.I, propaganda nonsense.

Going up the steps that lead into the Hospital William is pleading with Olivia.

"Please sweetheart Don`t do this I love you for what you are."

"What one of those freaky robots, no I want to put this to bed right now." Olivia goes to reception telling the receptionist.

"I want to see a Doctor right away, in privacy, whom do I say is requesting this."

"I`m Olivia of a dimension outside Earths domain and this is the super boy with powers that has been helping around Baltimore." Well the receptionist looks at Olivia as if she was looking at an Alien," Telling her.

"Bear with me for one minute, please take a seat while I make a phone call.

Olivia and William do take a seat and William holding Olivia's hand and looking at her and he could tell that the look on Olivia's face was one of a determined Woman. After about ten minutes this man in a white coat comes over to Olivia and William and introduces himself to them.

"Good morning My names Doctor Morris I`M a house Doctor hear at Baltimore Hospital, what seems to be the problem.

"Good morning Doctor my name is Olivia and
this is my fiancé William Drake the man with
superpowers."
"Oh yes I`ve heard a lot in the news about you.
What seems to be the matter with him."

"Nothing Doctor its just that he has a lot of
people telling him bad things about A.I Robots
and wanting to destroy them before they
advance to far."
"What nonsense, why we use a lot of A.I,
technology in our operating rooms, we would
not be able to do a lot of operations without
A.I. Technology, but please tell what I can do
to help with that."
"Well my boyfriend they have put it into his
head that I1m not a real human but one of
those Robots, I Would like you to examine me
and tell him what I`m made of. The Doctor
looking at Olivia in a way that said, Are you
real or what." He tells them.
"Right first of all ,we will arrange a full body
scam. That will tell us what your internal
organs are. "
Within two hours Olivia had had all of the tests
and it came to Doctor Morris telling them.
"Please will you join me in my Office I`ve all of
the results. Olivia and William go into his

Office and sit down with Doctor Morris opening his notes and telling them both.

"Right we have conducted a fully examination of One Olivia to determine her sex and what she consists off and I can confirm that our findings are that she is a health Woman and of course a human being and Sex a female."
William has the biggest grin and leans forward telling Olivia.
"I knew that all along, kissing her fully on the lips.

"But there is one thing I must stress to you."
This brought William back down to Earth saying.
"What's wrong Doctor please do tell.
"Congratulations Olivia is with child, you are pregnant."
"Well that was it, now both sat there and both William and Olivia sat there and their looks was total shock, then it turned to total joy.
In the Doctors Office he had French windows that were fully open Willian and Olivia stand up go over to the French windows Doctor and thank him and they go soaring off up into the ,
and go soaring up into clouds, with the Doctor shouting after them.

"Don't forget to be back for your check-ups
Olivia.

From that day on William had no more doubts
about Olivia and A.I. if the story does well
might be back with the rest of Olivia and
Williams life.

BY

JOHN BOLSTRIDGE